THE 10,000 CHILDREN THAT HITLER MISSED

Stories From The Kindertransport

LORI GRESCHLER

Copyright © 2009 Lori Greschler
All rights reserved.
Front cover picture of Lisa Seiden and her father.

ISBN: 1-4392-4333-6
ISBN-13: 9781439243336

Visit www.booksurge.com to order additional copies.

To learn more about the Holocaust please visit
www.holocaustkinder.com

"Know where you came from where you are going to, and for whom you will have to remember the account one day."
August 25, 1939, Chajor Gewurty (From Sonya's diary)

In memory of the children who were victims of the Holocaust, and for my daughter Cynthia Greschler. Words cannot describe my eternal love for you. You are filled with light. Cast your brightness upon us all.

ACKNOWLEDGEMENTS

I would like to express my gratitude to the survivors who contributed their stories. Their testimony represents a bridge to the past, a gift for the future, and a desire to eradicate racial and religious hatred. Thank you to the United States Memorial Holocaust Museum for access to the Photo Archive. Your support, knowledge, and excellent staff members are appreciated. I acknowledge the assistance of Anastasia Sierra for translating Sonja's diary from German to English. Your diligence is much appreciated.

I am grateful to Bertha Leverton and Andrea Goodmaker from the Kindertransport Association for providing me access to their files and allowing me to publish an ad in their newsletter. Thank you to Michele Decoteau, my editor, for providing a framework for the book without sacrificing its integrity. Lastly, to my family, thank you for holding my hand as I confronted the dark days of the Holocaust.

CONTENTS

Acknowledgements · · · · · · · · · · · · · · · · · iii
Preface · vii
History Of The Kindertransport · · · · · · · · xi

Chapter 1: Living With Royalty · · · · · · · · · · · · · · · · · 1
Chapter 2: A Childs Innocent Question · · · · · · · · · · · 15
Chapter 3: Inhumane Act Cast Upon The Parents · · · 19
Chapter 4: The Alpern Family: Twist Of Fate · · · · · · · 25
Chapter 5: A Sad Tale Of Missed Chances · · · · · · · · · 35
Chapter 6: Separated From My Parents For Half My Life · · · · · · · · · · · · · · · · · 41
Chapter 7: Torn Apart · 51
Chapter 8: Continuous Disarray · · · · · · · · · · · · · · · · 57
Chapter 9: Tormented On The Streets Of Munich · 61
Chapter 10: They Died I Survived! · · · · · · · · · · · · · · · · 65
Chapter 11: Thankful To Be Safe · · · · · · · · · · · · · · · · · 69
Chapter 12: The Diary Of Dirk · · · · · · · · · · · · · · · · · · 73
Chapter 13: The Journey For Life · · · · · · · · · · · · · · · · 87
Chapter 14: The Wassermann Family · · · · · · · · · · · · · 91
Chapter 15: Thirty Turbulent Months · · · · · · · · · · · · 95
Chapter 16: Schindler of Britain · · · · · · · · · · · · · · · · 103
Chapter 17: Sonya's Cherished Diary · · · · · · · · · · · · · 111

Timeline of Events · · · · · · · · · · · · · · · · · ·145

Postscript ·151

Picture Credits/Bibliography · · · · · · · · · 155

PREFACE

This manuscript is an anthology from the lives of children survivors during the inception of the Holocaust and World War II. Their chilling stories tell us what it was like for children to escape persecution and live in exile while their families remained trapped in Nazi territory and ultimately took their final breaths during the genocide of the twentieth century.

The Third Reich waged a war that almost eliminated the existence of Jews. Their systematic extermination and "final solution" sought to destroy an entire people in an effort to dominate the world. Even if we try to analyze the evil and demonic acts that transpired during those dark days, it is impossible to understand their logic. Sadly, in the end, the Jews and other targeted groups were murdered in every conceivable way known to mankind, from shootings to gassings to extreme neglect, starvation, and disease. Today, it is apparent that this terrible record of human atrocities will last until the end of time.

The seven boys and twelve girls featured in this collection describe their exile out of Europe on the Kindertransport and into the homes of strangers. Now in their late seventies, eighties, and nineties, they reveal what it was like during the rise and fall of the Nazi party. With trembling hands, fighting back tears and raw emotion, they reiterate their most painful memories.

In an effort to disenfranchise and separate the Jews from German society, new laws unfolded on a daily basis *(Nuremberg Laws)*, and curfews, boycotts, violence, exclusion from libraries, parks, and beaches, deprivation of their citizenship, and many other restrictions took hold. Once the chaos and prejudice began, the Jews were treated like outcasts. Lisa Seiden describes the shock of being forced out of her public school: "We wore the same kind of clothes, ate the same kind of food, played the same kind of games. There was no difference between us." However, the Third Reich would soon mark that difference. Alfred Terry, age eleven, even worn a swastika on his forearm in an effort to disguise his Jewish identity and buy food for his ailing father.

Excessive violence emerged, unconscionable tragedy prevailed, and the depths of oppression became catastrophic. Julius Fleischer recalls the day his father went out for a walk: "One day, he left the house to visit a friend and never returned. His body was later recovered in a nearby river and it was deemed suicide by drowning". No water was ever found in Mr. Fleischer's lungs. Friedel Kempler (Now Rita Weissman) remembers her father being arrested on November 9, 1938, a night known as Kristallnacht, "Without even a goodbye, a hug or a kiss; he left us that day and we never saw him again. He was later killed in the Nowy Sach ghetto." As time progressed, the children and their families realized that the history of their people, God's chosen ones, and the future of mankind would never be the same again.

In the end, the children belonged to a traumatized generation, and their faith and trust were overshadowed by separation, shame, and injustice. They were separated from their families unexpectedly to join the Kindertransport and forced to forge new identities and survive the trauma of separation and loss. After the greatest conflagration in human history and, the madness it left behind, the survivors wearily sifted through the rubble and found meaning in the ruins. Now we hear their testimonies, some for the very first time, and we learn about the anguish cast upon them from mankind.

The Kindertransport testimonies were compiled from London, Florida, Wisconsin, Washington, Toronto, Israel, Argentina, New Zealand and New York. The survivors have settled into happy lives all over the world despite their obvious turbulent years as children. Their stories are a reminder of what no child should ever have to endure. Holocaust survivor Ralph Mollerick describes the rescue: "It can be viewed as an act of kindness by the British government in saving 10,000 children, or it can be viewed as a cruel and inhumane act cast upon the parents by the Nazis for sending children unescorted to another land." As we read these accounts today, it is my hope that we learn to have empathy for the victims and possess a desire to fight prejudice and injustice whenever it crosses our path.

To preserve the authenticity and native language of the survivors, I have chosen not to correct their grammar, punctuation, and/or spelling in the interest of preserving their stories in a genuine manner. After decades of silence, the 10,000 Children That Hitler Missed finally Speak Out.

✲ ✲ ✲

HISTORY OF THE KINDERTRANSPORT

The Kindertransport (*children's transport*) was the largest and most successful rescue of endangered children from occupied Nazi territory during the outbreak of World War II. The children were forced to leave their parents behind while they traveled on a perilous journey to Great Britain in pursuit of freedom. Starting in December of 1938 and continuing for a nine month period, 10,000 predominately Jewish children traveled from Germany, Austria, Czechoslovakia, and Poland. The children were first transported by train and then ship from Berlin, Vienna, Prague, and many other cities in central Europe and ultimately brought into the Liverpool, Harwich station in Great Britain. The rescue was organized by The British Committee for the Jews of Germany along with The Movement for the Care of Children from Germany. They, along with countless volunteers, charitable organizations, and tireless workers rose to the occasion and organized the most remarkable rescue of the twentieth century. The British Foreign Minister Samuel Hoare pleaded with the British citizens to have sympathy and compassion for the Jews. He said, "Here is a chance of taking the young generation of a great people, here is a chance of mitigating to some extent the terrible suffering of their parents and their friends."

The rescue attempt was paramount because the Nazi regime was taking over Europe and organizing the most profound expression of anti-Semitism. Adolf Hitler was at the forefront of the mayhem. He was appointed chancellor of Germany on January 30, 1933 by President Paul Von Hindenberg and then named Fuhrer, or dictator. The Nazi Party occupied Germany under Adolf Hitler from 1933 to 1945 and governed under a totalitarian and autocratic ideology. Soon into his dictatorship, Nazi propaganda proliferated, and hostility toward Jews and non-Aryans developed. Initially, books were burned from Jewish authors to eradicate their literary accomplishments, and then Jewish-owned stores were boycotted and vandalized with anti-Semitic remarks. Jewish government workers were dismissed, eliminating their livelihood. By 1935, the Nuremberg laws were enacted, and a paper trail consisting of thousands of laws surfaced on a daily basis. These laws defined, humiliated, and cost Jews their livelihood. Towards the end of the war, the Nazi party organized a far reaching and complex death machine. Jews were placed in secluded ghettos or neighborhoods, railways for deportation were organized, and ultimately the horrendous concentration camps were put in place. Over a 12-year period, the Nazi party systematically murdered Jews, gypsies, homosexuals, Poles, Christians, the handicapped, Jehovah Witnesses, and other targeted groups, resulting in incomprehensible causalities.

The rescue attempt by the British government was frantically put in place after the terrible night that changed history books forever. In November 1938, a Polish student by the name of Herschel Grynszpan killed a German Diplomat in Paris name Ernest Von Rath. The murder was a spontaneous reaction to the expulsion of Polish citizens whose passports were revoked as a result of a new law passed by the Nazis. This event was utilized as a means to commence long planned attacks against the Jews.

On the night of November 9, 1938, Kristallnacht, The Night of Broken Glass, was staged by the Nazis. It was the most violent attack on the Jewish community in Germany and annexed Austria. In the middle of the night, thousands of Jewish homes, businesses, synagogues (Jewish Temples), and major department stores owned by Jews were ransacked, sledge hammered, bombed, set on fire, and destroyed.

Over 100 Jews were killed and thousands were subjected to horrible violence. Additionally, 30,000 Jewish men were forcibly sent to concentration camps. Fanny Bogdanow, a Kindertransport survivor, describes the account, "People now just say, 'Oh, the synagogues were burned down,' but they forget that the Germans broke into the Jewish homes, the windows and the window frames were hacked out, not a piece of furniture was left standing. They hacked holes in the walls, not a cup, not a saucer was left whole." Friedel Kempler, a Theresienstadt survivor recalls her father being arrested. "They came in our house in the middle of the night yelling, 'Get out, get out!' and they took my father, Joseph Kempler, and I never saw him again."

The violence of Kristallnacht fueled the rescue into high gear. In December of 1938, Lord Baldwine, Prime Minister of Britain, set up a plea to raise money for the rescue. Donations flooded in. Lord Baldwine was a compassionate leader who asked the following, "Think for a moment of the men, woman, and children who are being driven from their homes in Germany and Austria in a cruel persecution." They raised £550,000 (about $1,100,000 2007 US dollars) a great deal of money for the time. Subsequently, the delegation of British Jewish leaders appealed the Prime Minister of The United Kingdom, Neville Chamberlain. In the end, Britain ruled that they would accept an unspecified number of refugees under the age of seventeen. On November 21, 1938, the Kindertransport was launched. Subsequently, President Franklin Roosevelt organized the Evian conference to address the refugee crisis. It was attended by 31 countries, but the United States and most countries refused to accept the refugees. In the end, the world at large turned their backs on the Jews, and today they bear guilt for their decisions. Later in the war, the United States did accept approximately 1,000 families who were housed in Oswego, New York. However, as a whole, millions remained trapped.

Sir Samuel Hoare, then secretary of The Movement for the Care of Children from Germany, sped up the immigration process by issuing passports for groups of children as opposed to individual passports. Rules were placed upon the acceptance of children: every child had to guarantee a £50 bond (about $1,500 US dollars) care for their education, housing and their journey back home when the war was over. The children with sponsors were sent to live with their prospective family while the children without sponsors lived in hostels or facilities that could care for groups of children. Some lived on farms or were sent to boarding schools, and others were taken as domestics. About 5,000 of the children lived in foster homes. Hundreds of offers from volunteers were received from every religious denomination welcoming the children with open arms.

On December 1, 1938, the first transport from Berlin left, and the children embarked on a trip that saved their lives. Nine days later, another train departed and soon a few hundred children were led to safety. After several months, the rescue efforts concentrated on Austria and shifted away from Germany. When the German army attacked parts of Czechoslovakia, a hasty plan was devised to transport children from Prague in March of 1939. By February 1939, Jewish children from Poland were rescued. Once the trains entered Belgium or the Netherlands, they continued their voyage by ship. Approximately twice a week for a nine-month period, children arrived by sea. The last group of children to be rescued departed on September 1, 1939, the day Poland was invaded and Great Britain, France, and other countries officially entered the war.

The children entered a country that was foreign to them. The customs and language were different and they had to adjust to living without the love and support of their natural parents and the familiarity of their once comfortable lives. Many British families welcomed the children and tried to ease their adjustment slowly and compassionately. The children struggled to understand the enormity of the events unfolding around them.

Most just clung to the memory of their parents and happily anticipated their reunion after the war.

Although the children left to evade the Nazi regime, they soon found themselves in the clutches of war in Great Britain as well. On September 3, 1939, England and France declared war on Germany. An earlier agreement was made with Poland that England and France would defend them if the Germans attacked. That agreement was honored on September 1, 1939, when Hitler's army marched into Poland, and, two days later, the war broke out.

The children had to be evacuated at once. They packed their suitcases and were taken by train to the countryside where they would live with yet another family. Subsequently, the Germans ravaged London with bombs and destroyed many historic buildings as well as demolishing neighborhoods. Many people were killed and seriously wounded, but the refugees were unharmed.

The children yearned for the war to end and to reestablish their lives. After six years of living without their families, on May 8, 1945, V-E Day was officially declared, and the British were relieved that the war was finally over. All of Europe was elated. The enormous destruction, mass killings, and injustice of the war could never be repaired.

The Holocaust ravaged all of Europe and nearly destroyed the lives and accomplishments of the Jewish people and other targeted groups. Subsequently, Adolf Hitler committed suicide. During his reign, he managed to kill millions, including at least 1.5 million children, but the rescued children from the Kindertransport all survived. *They Were The 10,000 Children Hitler Missed!*

The end of the war brought the reality that many of the children's parents had been murdered. Most of their parents were sent to the gas chambers and had died. Out of the 10,000 children rescued, approximately, 60% lost their parents. Although the "Kinders" were fortunate to have survived the Holocaust themselves, they endured undue suffering at the hands of the Nazis. Not only did they lose their parents, they also mourned the loss of their relatives and friends, and homes. In the end, we all nearly lost, one thousand years of rich culture, tradition and Jewish religion.

Losing a loved one in a time of genocide creates a sense of unjust guilt. The absence of their parents created a deep rooted loneliness and grief that tormented them for the rest of their lives. Mrs. Dorothy Hardisty, executive director of the Movement for the Care of Children, describes the refugees, "The mental and emotional suffering the children had endured was appalling. It was not only that at short notice they were torn from the places they knew: it was not only that suddenly they were bereft of all sense of security-these blows had been preceded by long periods of unhappiness and fear."

Approximately one quarter of the children immigrated to Canada or the United States while others went to Israel or became British citizens and lived the rest of their lives in the country that had rescued them from the perils of war.

✡ ✡ ✡

Lisa Seiden and her father before the Holocaust. Lisa left on the Kindertransport at age nine and was reunited with her parents eight years later. (Courtesy Lisa Seiden)

CHAPTER 1: LIVING WITH ROYALTY

Lisa Seiden is a young, curly-haired, and charming Jewish girl filled with wit and personality. Her older brother, Peter, is a brown-eyed, delightful boy with an inquisitive mind and a good-natured heart. They were born into a wealthy family in Vienna, Austria shortly before Hitler took power, and they appreciated a life of find culture. Their mother passionately enjoyed Beethoven and Wagner and played the piano with zeal. She possessed an unheralded love for the arts. Their father earned his Ph. D. in Chemical Engineering and was born into a poor family in which he learned the ethics of hard work. He was a solider in WWI and caught tuberculosis, which is often deadly, but he possessed a fortitude that enabled him to go on living despite only having half of one of his lungs intact. He is described as follows, "My father was a tenacious fighter. Introverted by nature, his greatest gift was an unflinching perseverance, a character which helped him overcome the many adversities he came up against during his life."

Lisa and Peter's lives were filled with happy memories and bursting with childhood fun, family gatherings, and lavish affairs. Suddenly, their lives started to change. First, a curfew forbade Jews to be on the streets after 6:00 P.M. The children were forced out of their schools, their household books were confiscated, and their father was arrested and deported by the Nazis. By order of the Gestapo (secret police), their mother was pushed into the streets and ordered to scrub the sidewalks with a hand-brush on her bare knees as onlookers laughed and grinned at the Jews scrubbing the words "Jewish Swine" off the cement.

By December of 1938, the Seiden family decided to send their children, Lisa and Peter, to England in an effort to shield them from the daily persecution and violence perpetrated against the Jews. The bright-eyed youngsters traveled by train then ship and arrived in England three days later. They spent a short time in a transit camp then lived with a sponsor named Mrs. Tanner, a prominent figure in the community who owned a 26-room mansion. When Mrs. Tanner was contemplating moving out of England, Lisa was placed with the Emperor of Abissinia (Ethiopia), Haile Selassie. Mr. Selassie fled Abissinia in

1: Living with Royalty

May of 1936 when fascist Italy invaded his country. Lisa felt like a little princess because she dined with an Emperor and two princesses and rubbed elbows with many dignitaries. She ultimately left the Selassie house because she desperately wanted to reside with her brother, who had not been invited to live with the royal family. In the interim, her parents managed to flee to South America. After an eight year separation from their parents, Lisa and Peter finally left England and were reunited with their parents in South America in 1946.

On a day just like any other, on going into class my teacher called me aside and kneeling down, looked straight at me and I noticed that there were tears in her eyes. Then she held me in her arms and kissed me. Finally she said, "Go home, you can't be here any more, go and don't come back." I remember my confusion, as the tears on her cheeks did not coincide with the terrible words she had just spoken. Even though I was already nine, I couldn't grasp the meaning of what had just happened and tried to remember what I had done wrong, if I had lacked respect in any way or had made a problem for anyone. But when I asked her why, she repeated the hard words in a soft voice, "Go home and ask your mother, she will know how to explain this!" she added. Then, taking me by the hand, she led me to the door of the school.

In front of my mother, I waited for an answer to my question. She fell into a chair, took her head into her hands as if in pain and closed her eyes. After some moments she said, "It's because we are Jews." Had she said that it was because of my curly hair or the color of my eyes, my surprise could not have been greater, as the fact of being an Austrian child of Jewish decent had had, until that moment, the same importance for me and nothing in my appearance, manner or life style had made me feel different from the other children at my school. We wore the same kind of clothes, ate the same kind of food, played the same kind of games. There was no difference between us. But soon the things which were happening around us, took care to "mark the difference" and the punishment of not being able to continue in my school was but the first, followed by others, deeper, darker and completely irreparable.

A friend of the family named Mrs. Bauer informed my mother that the Gestapo was looking for my father. Our mother told us that our father had hidden himself below the small bridge near our house. We, the children, knew the place well as we used to enjoy climbing up to this secret hollow, surrounded by dense vegetation, and pretend that we were hiding out in some deep, green cave. My mother decided that I should take him the food, as she considered me to be the least conspicuous member of the family. I still remember clearly the many instructions I received:

* I had to climb over a wall at the back of the garden, making sure before jumping into the street that no one was there to see me.

* "Don't run, just skip" my mother instructed me. This was the fastest way of advancing without causing suspicion, at least for little girls.

1: Living with Royalty

* If anyone greeted me on the way, I had to return the greeting, or if necessary, stop a moment to exchange a word or two.

* If I came across any SS troops, I had to go on normally but making sure that no one was following me.

* Once I was near the bridge, I had to stop, look cautiously around, pretend to be playing, wait until there was no one in sight and finally climb up to the hiding place as quickly as possible.

* Even more important than the food I had in the knapsack on my back, were the many messages I had to keep in mind. My mother took pains to make the importance of this clear to me. "I cannot write them down for you, it's too dangerous, you must memorize them and repeat them to "papa", he must know that I am doing everything to get the permit so that we can all leave the country as soon as possible."

The encounter with my father in that cold, dark burrow under the bridge will remain engraved like tongues of flame in the back of my mind, impossible to be forgotten. Sometimes I still see him in my dreams, just as he was then. He, sitting there, desolate; and I would throw myself into his arms, not understanding, not believing what was happening. He would console me, saying that he was proud of me, that I was a good girl that I had to be strong, that all would be well. But nothing, absolutely nothing turned out well, as the Gestapo caught him a few days later and he was deported to Dachau, a concentration camp somewhere in Germany. I remember that I was so distressed when my mother told me what had happened that I didn't want to know when and how it had occurred, but only why, why, why.... Eight long years passed before I saw him again.

On December 17, 1938, I, along with my brother Peter, were leaving the country on the Kindertransport. We were going to England. My mother told me, "It is necessary for us to part for some time, but I want you and Peter to stay together, come what may. Don't get separated, I count on you for that, you must stay together." She made me promise this again and again amongst kisses and embraces.

Here is an excerpt from Peter's diary on that day.

Vienna
The great day has come. We are all very excited. In the morning we had to say goodbye to all our friends. All of them almost cried. Around midday, we went to our grandmother's house to have lunch. She gave me a four-leaf clover in the afternoon and told me it would bring me luck in my life. She said that she had had it since she was ten years old, now she is 63. I will take good care of it.

We had to be at the station at 9 PM Mother, Aunt Trude, Aunt Lily and Kurt also came. We went to the station by car. We were taken into a big hall where there were many other children standing around. After half an hour the parents had to say

1: Living with Royalty

goodbye to their children. Many cried. We didn't as we didn't take it so seriously. The train didn't leave Vienna until two o'clock in the morning, seven hours after it should have.

We initially stayed at the Dovercourt Harwich holiday camp which was utilized as a transit camp for the refugees. Then a gracious Canadian lady named Mrs. Tanner took us into her home. We arrived in Bath a city in the south of England.

Because of bureaucratic paper work, I was only able to go to my first class in my new school on the 19th of January 1939, two weeks later than the other children. The school was called St. Mark's [and the] Tanner's house, was just a ten minute walk away. On that first day, which was cold, white clear and sunny, I felt very excited and happy. I was wearing a thick pair of black rubber boots, which Mrs. Tanner had bought for me as she considered the ones I had brought from Vienna, short, thin with two fasteners on the side, inadequate for the low temperatures reigning at that moment in England. "What would your mother say if you caught a cold," she said between gestures and laughter. As I didn't have the dark grey skirt, white blouse and navy blue cardigan yet, the uniform of the school, I wore my sailor dress with the big square collar and my white woolen stockings and of course the black boots which reached my knees.

I remember how all the children turned round and stopped talking when I walked into the classroom for the first time. As I didn't know where to sit, the teacher came to fetch me and took me with her to the front of the class. Standing beside me, she put one hand on my head and said, "Lisa!" and then pointed at a boy, sitting in the front row who stood up and said, "Nestor" and sat down again. In this way, in quick succession, the children introduced themselves until it was a girl's turn, who instead of standing up and saying her name, burst into tears and ran toward me, throwing her arms around my neck and letting off little squeaks of emotion. This broke the ice, and others followed and we were all arms and legs, laughing and crying. From that moment on, I was accepted, protected and spoiled.

Later, much later when I was able to understand enough English, I was told that the teacher had been talking extensively to her pupils about the "poor little girl" who was going to be with them this term. She told me that this girl had been torn away from her parents, thrown out of her school, forced to leave her country, her way of life. She talked to them about the injustice of racial discrimination, about the Nazis and how a terrible war was raging across Europe.

It was the month of January 1939 and the free world, including England, began to "observe" the belligerent advances of the German troops. The imminent of war could be felt in the air. Mrs. Tanner had two sons who lived in Canada. When England stopped being a safe country to live in and fear grew, they begged their mother to emigrate and join Canada as soon as possible. In such times, making vital decisions quickly becomes indispensable and Mrs. Tanner resolved to sell the house and leave. Mrs. Tanner, who was acquainted with many important people, tried to find a new home for

1: Living with Royalty

us. Amongst her friends was the Emperor of Abissinia, Haille Selassie, called Negus.

One day a representative of the royal family came to visit us. He arrived with a princess and with her wooly white dog, named Lulu. Sometimes they stayed overnight, so we got to know each other quite well. One day the princess invited me to her home, but the invitation did not include my brother, a fact which did not dissuade me from going.

On January 28, 1939 this is what I wrote to my father:

I have some very, very good news. I wrote mama that the representative of the king of Abissinia came to visit us and now the Princess of Abissinia is living with us and she said that she's going to take me with her when she goes back to her home, but not to Abissinia. She wants me to go with her for some days, but without Peter. That doesn't matter, does it? I'd like to go, wouldn't I?

I'm looking forward to seeing the King, the two princesses and the prince and all the officers. Anyway, all the royal family. The princess asked me to sing and dance, she would like to see me. I know a little because I have a friend who is as good as Koller, so good and she knows how to dance and she is going to teach me.

A few days later, we set off for the Emperor's house. Mrs. Tanner waving goodbye and Peter standing a bit further back, looking a bit angry. He too would have liked to go to "The house of a King". Sitting in the back of a big black car beside a princess, already made me feel like a queen, to say the least when all the servants bowed at our passing on walking up the wide, marble stairs leading up to the entrance of a palace. I was taken into a princely room. As my royal playmate, Haile Selassie's son, was not at home, I had time to look around. In the middle of the room, an enormous bed under a bluish satin awning like roof with the family insignia embroidered in the centre. This was repeated on the bed-cover. In one corner there was another smaller bed which, so I found out later, was for the Prince's nanny.

But the arrival of my supposed companion made me forget everything else. There he was, a sight to see! His dark skin contrasting with the cream-coloured suit he was wearing. With a friendly white smile, he put his little brown hand in mine and, walking very upright, led me to his playroom. There he showed me all his toys, making demonstrations of how this tank rolled forward or that plane could really fly. We enjoyed ourselves until "his" suppertime, which was served at 6 o'clock. I, as a full-grown 9-year-old, was allowed to join the adults in the big living room.

The Negus came to say goodnight to his little son and invited me to follow him. We went into a very ornately decorated room, which was full of people. I remember white teeth in dark faces, silky embraces and strong perfumes. They asked me to play something on the piano and I played "Para Elisa," the only thing I remembered.

During dinner I sat next to Haile Selassie. Every now and then, he leaned towards me and said some friendly word. The others smiled at us or spoke amongst

1: Living with Royalty

themselves. Soup, in big silver bowls was served and as it looked very hot, I decided to wait a bit. I noticed some little platters beside the bigger plates, on which there were some small honey coloured rolls. As I had nothing to do, I forked one of them and put it into my mouth. My host whispered in my ear, "Don't eat it like that, it's butter for the bread." After that I was more careful and ate only after I had seen how others did it.

Here is a letter to my parents about my royal visit.

Dear good sweet papa and mama
2nd February 1939

Now I want to tell you something really nice! The princess asked me if I wanted to go home with her. I said yes, of course. So a quarter of an hour later, we got into a taxi, but without Peter. A minister drove the car and we arrived in a very big garden and then the palace. There was velvet on the stair and the lady servants and the men servants bowed before us. Then I was taken into a room. The beds were covered with light blue silk bed-covers. This room was for a king. I had to wait a tiny bit with Lulu, the dog because the little prince was just invited out for tea, but he arrived later with his nurse. You have never seen such an enchanting boy, black hair, brown skin and white trousers which made him look so nice.

He asked my name and so on and 10 minutes later, we went to his room, it was a quarter to five, and played and had fun. In the meantime the nurse prepared his supper. He must go to sleep at six, I, at nine. I can't remember what we had for supper, but it was very good. I have a lovely room and big, just for me. I told the nurse to leave the door open, in that way I won't be afraid. I slept like a log. I can't write so much, my hand is aching. We also had a good breakfast and played all day. I saw the king and all the family. It was wonderful. How nice of the princess to invite me! Not many people can see the King of Abissinia. It is late at night, I will write at another moment. Lisa

The days passed and I quickly got used to the luxury, to the food, to the cuddly bed, to the maternal nanny and above all to my lively playmate for whom I was "big" and he was small." Peter, who was supposed to follow me, didn't come, but that didn't worry me. I told him everything on the phone and we thought that we were going to be together again very soon. At some moment during the day, the Negus and his wife would come round to see us. He always asked me if I liked his house, if I felt well and if I felt happy.

Sometimes he stayed for a while and played with his son. Thrown on the carpet, the little one would fight him, jumping all over him, pulling his beard, shouting and laughing. I never joined in thoses games and clearly remember sitting between two huge dolls, imitations of the Buckingham Palace Guards. I had never seen such big dolls, they were taller than the prince and imposing in their red uniform, gold buttons and tall fuzzy black hats which covered their eyes. When many years later, I saw the real ones, standing like statues, rifles on their shoulders doing their duty before the Queen's Palace, a warm memory returned of the two unforgettable "just as big" ones in Haile Selassie's house.

1: Living with Royalty

But my brother didn't come, and I began to ask [for] him with more insistence. They assured me that he would turn up soon. In the end, I realized that he wasn't going to join me and one night in the darkness of my bed, I found myself crying. The next morning I didn't feel like having breakfast, at lunchtime I didn't want to eat and in the evening I wasn't hungry, they became alarmed put their hands on my forehead and asked me if I was feeling sick. But I didn't say anything. The Negus came with his wife. She didn't speak German but was always very nice to me. When he wanted to know why I wasn't eating, I surprised myself by asking the same question again: "When will my brother come?"

In spite of the tears of the little one, I was taken back to Mrs. Tanner's house. I was taken back to my brother. I will never know how my life would have been, had I stayed in the house of Haile Selassie, without my brother.

Lisa and Peter were once again reunited. Mrs. Tanner realized that to separate them would cause undue emotional harm. They continued to live with Mrs. Tanner for several weeks but she ultimately sold her house and moved to Canada. On March 25, 1939, the children moved in with the Hole family. The family had six children and lived on a farm. From day one, they felt an immediate kinship with the children and considered them instant siblings. Lisa soon called Mrs. Hole "Mum" and they developed an everlasting bond. Lisa describes the Hole family: "I lived in her house and became one of the family, forgetting that she really was not my mother nor her children my brothers and sister. I knew, but I didn't want to know that one day I would have to leave. But that day always seemed far away, forgotten in my daily life." In 1942, Lisa and Peter left England and everything to which they had become accustomed. Lisa arrived on the Kindertransport at age nine. Over the next eight years, she blossomed into a woman and was no longer the same little girl who had arrived. Tearing her away from her adopted family was very painful. Lisa was completely distraught at the thought of leaving, yet beyond the horizon were her birth parents anxiously awaiting to see their bright-eyed children once again. However, somewhere along the path of her complex life, Lisa admits that subconsciously she slowly substituted her parents with the Hole family and really wanted to spend the rest of her life with them.

*Lisa's story is dedicated to her wonderful grandchildren, Matthew, Sebastian and Allen who has brought her so much love and joy.

Children peeking out of the train window as they leave Germany while in route to England on the Kindertransport. (Courtesy USHMM)

CHAPTER 2: A CHILD'S INNOCENT QUESTION

Anita Hoffer was born in Berlin, Germany on June 6, 1933 to an affluent Jewish family. Her parents divorced when she was three and Anita and her mother went to live with her grandparents, Omi and Oma. She recalled packing her little suitcase to visit her father at her paternal grandparents' home. "I enjoyed those visits because my cousins were there and always made a fuss over me." The political turmoil did not escape her thoughts because young Anita was given the local news by her cousins.

The 10,000 Children That Hitler Missed

"I heard them talking about the Jewish taxes, deportation, and having to leave the public school and leave their Gentile (non Jewish) friends." In June of 1939, shortly after her sixth birthday, Anita asked her grandmother a question that would change her destiny for the rest of her life.

In those days we had no televisions, computers or cell phones. The radio was full of propaganda and my family wanted to keep me naïve so I had no idea what was going on in Berlin at the time. When I would visit my cousins however, I got a glimpse into the turmoil that was unfolding. The restrictions unfolded on a daily basis and soon my cousins were forced to leave their public school because they were Jewish.

In June 1939 after Kristallnacht, which destroyed my grandparent's furniture store, I was still going to kindergarten. My grandmother, Omi, picked me up after school and took me to her apartment house. We waited at the elevator with the other tenants then we entered. I asked, "Omi, Why do you hate Mr. Hitler?" You could hear a pin drop in the elevator if anyone reported this remark to the authorities my whole family would be killed. Oma answered, "I don't hate Mr. Hitler," at that moment we arrived on our floor Oma grabbed my hand and ran for our apartment and called for Opi. He saw Oma's face and sent me to my room. I had no idea what I had done so I started to cry and listened at the door to their conversation. Oma repeated over and over again, "We have to get rid of her before she gets us all killed." I fell asleep and when I awoke Oma and mother were with me and told me that I was never to speak again to

2: A Child's Innocent Question

anyone outside the family and I was not to go to school anymore. They did not explain. A few weeks later I awoke to mother packing my little suitcase, she refused to answer my questions and just told me to get dressed and come to the kitchen for breakfast. I did and Oma and Opa joined us, no one ate but me. Finally Oma said we have to leave, I said where? No one answered me. Mother took me to the rail road station; there were many children and parents. The train arrived, my mother put me on the train (which I found out later was unusual) and I sat down and looked around. When I turned back to my mother she was gone! I had no idea who would take care of me or where I was going.

I lived with a Russian family for several months but was beaten up regularly by the English kids until I got rid of my German accent. My mother arrived in England and got a job as a housekeeper but was fired because she was a lousy housekeeper. My mother placed me in an orphanage to find work. Once again, nobody wanted me. An affluent woman named Miss Scott showed up at the orphanage one day and asked if I wanted to live with her. She had never married but loved children. She had a houseful of kids. Most were refugees from the English countryside. She was very strict. We had to be good, tell the truth, go to school. All the good things. There wasn't a bad kid among us. We were scared. We didn't want to leave Miss Scott.

Anita's mother returned with visas and they traveled to the United States. Anita remembers the trip, "We were on the last ship leaving London, and this was in November just before

Pearl Harbor. I was lucky in every possible way." Her father and his new wife fled to Shanghai, but their lives were difficult there. Her mother hid the fact that Anita was going on the Kindertransport because her father would never have agreed to her departure. Luckily, she fled. Anita currently lives in Boca Raton, Florida and is a buyer and merchandise manager for Bloomingdales. She also heads the Kindertransport Association regional chapter in Florida.

Ralph Mollerick age 8 and his sister Edith age 17 pose for this portrait prior to going on the Kindertransport. (Courtesy Ralph Mollerick)

CHAPTER 3: INHUMANE ACT CAST UPON THE PARENT

Ralph Mollerick and his older sister, Edith, fled Wolfhager, Germany in 1938 on the Kindertransport. Ralph was eight and Edith was seventeen. Ralph recalls his parents Josef and Selma saying, "We will all be reunited in a few months." Young and naïve, Ralph thought, "It would be a lot of fun to go." Unfortunately, his parents promise to be reunited again never came true. Ralph struggles with deep-rooted sadness today at the thought of his parents being trapped in Germany and ultimately being murdered by the Nazis. He describes the

The 10,000 Children That Hitler Missed

Kindertransport, "It can be viewed as an act of kindness by the British government in saving 10,000 children, or it can be viewed as a cruel and inhumane act cast upon the parents by the Nazis for sending children unescorted to another land." Ralph and Edith Mollerick reveal their story of triumph and separation.

Early one morning, my father told me that my sister and I would be taking a trip to England. He informed me that in three months we would be reunited and then all of us would sail to American. Two days later, my parents took us to the train station in Hamburg, Germany. It was very large and many people were standing with their children hearing last minute instructions from their parents. My mother, with tears in her eyes, spoke to my sister Edith, to take care of your little brother. She handed Edith a prayer book and asked her to remember your parents and grandparents in her prayers. My father pulled me over to his side and said that I should get an education as this is one thing no one can take away from you.

As I recall, our parents were not allowed to take us to the track where the train was waiting. We each had one small suitcase, and as we turned to leave, I could see my parents with outstretched arms crying and wondering if this would be the last time they would see us. We were given a card with a number which hung from our neck, and we were told to go to the train. Once on the train, we were instructed that all shades must be pulled down. I peeped from under the shade to see if I could see my parents. Unfortunately, there was no sign of them.

3: Inhumane Act Cast Upon The Parent

The train deported. Little did we know where we were going. As the train picked up speed, the rhythm of the tracks seemed to clank, we're leaving, we're leaving, we're leaving. The train took us to a boat. I recalled two little girls in front of me on the gangplank. The older one was carrying a doll, and the younger one had a night potty hanging over her shoulder. I don't remember anything else about the boat ride over to England.

It was January 1939, and a cold day in England. We were taken to Dovercourt, a summer camp for children. The bunks had no heating and we all huddled together to keep warm. By nighttime, the temperature had fallen to −12C. It was the coldest night of the year and I recall cuddling up to my sister and fell asleep. In the morning, we were told how the camp operates. One of the instructors emphasized that the way out of the camp is to learn English and she drilled me all day, until in three weeks I could speak English.

My sister and I were eager to get out of the camp. Edith called a girlfriend who lived in London. She went with her and I was placed in a boy's hostel. I hated my new accommodations, but it was better than camp.

During the war years, I was moved from hostel-to-hostel and each time further north where the bombings were fewer. I often thought of my parents who promised to join us. In 1942, the International Red Cross notified me that my parents were taken to Lodz, Poland, a holding ghetto for Jews prior to shipment to Auschwitz. I never saw my parents again.

Ralph Mollerick moved to Washington in 1964 and headed the Washington chapter for the Kindertransport Association.

He took his father's last words to heart and pursued his education. Ralph was a mechanical engineer for NASA (National Aeronautical and Space Administration) for 33 years. He was instrumental in designing and building satellites utilized for providing images for meteorologists. In 1987, Edith passed away due to muscular dystrophy. Ralph was her caretaker, and their bond was everlasting. When Edith became ill, she gave Ralph the prayer book. Ralph retired in 2006 and currently lives in Florida.

*Upon arrival at Dovercourt all newcomers, including Ralph Mollerick were given rules to follow, "Advice To Refugees."

"Remember in the first place that you are guests in this country and not its owners. Act therefore with the courtesy of guests. It will help you in your contacts with the English people if you remember the following rules:

Speak English if you can–if you cannot, do not talk German loudly in public. The English people are a quiet race. They do not like loud talkers and loud conversations in German at this time is at all costs to be avoided.

(1) In the same way avoid gesticulation in public. The English people are unemotional- at any rate on the surface- and anything theatrical or dramatic offends them.
(2) Take particular care not to push yourself forward in shops. There are ample supplies of food and

3: Inhumane Act Cast Upon The Parent

clothing in the country. Take your turn, ask for no more than your due rations and the English shopkeeper will treat you fairly and courteously.

(3) Do not try to barter about prices. The English shopkeepers have fixed prices-in many important articles fixed by the Government-and it gives offense that they are too high.

(4) Refugees often give offense, mainly through ignorance, by taking positions out of their turn in queues at train stops, ticket offices and theatres. Take your place at the extreme end of the queues and wait your turn-the English love fair play.

(5) Do not criticize England or the English. Do not explain how truthfully, that certain things are much better managed in Germany. The English are quite capable and ready to do their own criticism of their Government and institutions.

(6) The English people have freely and liberally given you a place of refuge. Show them by your courtesy to others, your consideration for all people, your kindness, that they have justified in their generosity."

The Alpern family arrived as a complete intact family on the Kindertransport after a long journey that lasted many days. February 15, 1939 (Courtesy Renee Moss)

CHAPTER 4: THE ALPERN FAMILY - TWIST OF FATE

The Alpern family grew up in the Black Forest region of Germany and shared a prosperous life. In the fall of 1938, Poland passed a law that required all Polish Jews living abroad for more than five years to return to Poland to have their passport stamped. The stamping had to be carried out by a certain date (within two weeks) or the bearer would lose citizenship. The Nazis realized that Germany would be filled with thousands of stateless Jews. In response, they forcibly sent the Polish Jews out of Germany and back into Poland, where their passports originated. Roughly 15,000 Jews were arrested and sent to the Polish border. Upon arrival, the Polish government rejected their admittance and they were stuck in a country that no longer recognized them as citizens. The Alpern family was one of the 15,000 stateless Jews. With only a small sum of money and one suitcase each, the family was left with four children to support in the middle of nowhere. They walked to the small town of Zbaszyn on the boarder between Poland and Germany. They lived in a refugee camp, but the conditions were inhumane and many could not endure the conditions. Some died while others committed suicide.

Henry, the eldest brother, recalls the sleeping arrangements at the refugee camp in the fall of 1938, "We all slept in a barn upstairs, we later had our own barn. There was one bed, with a straw mattress, Mum and Dad slept on one end, and Henry, Sonja, and Anita slept on the other end. I slept in a box of some sort, cardboard or wooden, I'm not sure." They lived on hard-boiled eggs and bread. The second oldest, Anita, remembers walking with Henry one day and meeting a farmer who shared the fact that he was slaughtering a pig the next day. He offered them a wurscht. Anita recalls her mother's reaction, "When we took it 'home' our mother refused to let us eat it because it was pork." Although they were hungry, many Jews do not eat pork or any meat that is not kosher. Kosher meat is blessed by a Rabbi and slaughtered under Rabbinical supervision.

4: The Alpern Family - Twist of Fate

Another family, the Grynspans, simultaneously occupied the camp. Their son, Herschel Grynspan, age 17, was residing in Paris when he received word that his parents had been forced out of their home. Their belongings were confiscated and they were living in the camp with their citizenship revoked. Out of sheer rage, he went to the German Embassy filled with anger with the idea to shoot the German Ambassador of France despite the consequences. Actually, he shot the secretary, Ernest Roth Rath, because the Ambassador was not in the Embassy at the time. Mr. Rath later died, and the Nazis used this event to fuel their planned attacks against the Jews. Thus, the pogrom called Kristallnacht, or The Night of Broken Glass, emerged. Some scholars believe this event was actually the start of the Holocaust. The violence resulted in widespread persecution, arrests, and devastating destruction.

As violence was soaring across Europe, the Alpern family received some luck amongst the turmoil. In the winter of 1939, the family was permitted to go to England on the Kindertransport. Remarkably, they were the only complete family to flee to England via the Kindertransport. That decision saved their lives.

My story is different from so many stories of kinder who were saved from Nazi Germany thanks to the Kindertransport. My mother Adèle, née Antmann, grew up in Zurich in Switzerland and my father Leo Alpern although born and bred in Berlin, held a Polish passport -his parents having originated from Poland- and they had never been eligible for German naturalisation. Both my parents were born in 1903 and brought up in orthodox Jewish homes.

I was the youngest of four children. I was born in Freiberg in 1937 and my name was Irena. My siblings were Sonja (born in 1935, also in Freiburg), Anita (born in 1933 in Zurich) and Heinrich (born in 1931 in Zurich). We lived in Freiburg, which is a beautiful university city in the black forest. My father ran his own drapery business and we observed a fully traditional Jewish life. My father was proud to live in Germany and until his dying day he could never understand how the German people, were brainwashed by Hitler and his ilk.

Under a Bill of March 31st 1938, Polish passports would be revoked if their bearers had lived abroad for more than five years. The Germans realized that this Polish Bill was aimed at the Jews. After the law took effect on October 31st 1938 the Germans would risk being left with 15,000 stateless Jews whom no country would admit. To avoid this danger, 15,000 men, women and children were rounded up, herded into railway stations with just one piece of luggage each and 10 marks to travel the night of 29/30th to the German/Polish border. The men had all been taken to prison the night before where many refused to eat the prison food because of the laws of kashrut.

In October 1938 my father was arrested and taken to prison along with other Polish Jews living in Freiburg. Within days our family had to leave our home in Germany for a refugee transit camp in Zbonszyn on the Polish/German borders. Our whole family shared a small room with another family. Conditions in Zbonszyn were desperate and there were many suicides.

4: The Alpern Family - Twist of Fate

My maternal grandmother, on hearing of our plight and subsequent arrival at Zbonszyn, wrote immediately from Switzerland where she lived with her sister in Poland begging her to help us and take us into her home. Her sister sent us some chickens but said she was unable to take us in – I suppose through fear – not everyone had strength of mind or character sufficient for such occasions. Yet fate had been kind to us for sadly my grandmother's sister and all her family were killed along with so many other Polish Jews.

A plea was also issued to the Swiss authorities to allow our family to travel to Switzerland but they replied that they would not admit my father and so my mother refused to leave him. It was as an act of revenge on hearing of his own parents' deportation to Zbonszyn, that Herschel Grynszpan shot a German diplomat in Paris – an act that the Germans used as a pretext to launch on November 10th the Kristallnacht pogrom (sometimes known as the night of the broken glass, when Jewish shop windows were smashed and synagogues set on fire).

Just as the spirit of my parents began to sink still lower, my brother aged seven and my two sisters aged five and three received permission to go to England. Unknown names had stood as guarantors for us. My parents knew that they might never see them again but were prepared to sacrifice their own feelings in order to save them the miseries of the camp. Other Jewish refugees criticized them for letting the children go but they felt sure that - however difficult a decision – it was the right one to make.

Then, some days after my brother and sisters had left the camp my parents received some amazing news. Because I was a baby and dependent on my mother they too were to be allowed to travel to England as domestic servants. So ended over three months at Zbonszyn.

My parents and I journeyed to Gdanya by train not knowing that by some extraordinary coincidence my brother and sisters were travelling on the same train. It was not until my mother looked up and suddenly saw Anita, my elder sister, walking down the corridor hand in hand with an elder girl that our good fortune became apparent.

And so it was that we all crossed to England on the S.S. Warszawa on February 15th 1939 to start our new life in England. Waiting to greet that Kindertransport of 56 Jewish refugees at Cotton Wharf in London were journalists and photographers from the British Press. Our family was featured in many of the newspapers as we were the only complete family to have traveled via Kindertransport.

There is a photograph of my sister Sonja and of me sitting on the lap of Mr. George Lansbury, an eminent politician, entitled "Love and Suffering." The caption reads: This is not merely a picture of youth and age. It is one of love and suffering. The two little kiddies Mr. George Lansbury has on his knees are two of the fifty-four refugee children who arrived in London from no-man's land in Zbonszyn last week. The younger child is still afraid even of the photographer and not even Mr. Lansbury, who has gained the respect of the world

4: The Alpern Family - Twist of Fate

for his huanitarianism can yet make the other one smile."

On arrival in London we were taken to the Jews' temporary shelter where my parents remained for some short while. Heinrich (later known as Henry), Anita and Sonja were evacuated to families in Golders Green in London and I was sent to a children's home in Watford in Hertfordshire. A Quaker family, named Ponsford, hearing of our plight, offered us the use of their house in Canvey Island in Essex and for a short while we were once again living together as a family.

Once war broke out all aliens, even friendly aliens, were moved away from London. Once again my siblings were evacuated – this time to Paignton in Devon. My parents requested that they too should be moved to Devon in order to be able to visit their children.

In 1942 my younger brother Elliot was born – thus we proudly added a British member to our family! Sadly, he died of an asthma attack in 1961 when he was just 18 years old. An ambulance had been called but when it arrived the oxygen cylinders it carried were empty! No words can fully describe the pain that we all felt at his death. This baby had been our symbol of hope and of a new life and we all cherished him.

In 1943 our whole family moved to Torquay in Devon and I lived there until I left school at the age of 18 and came to London to study languages at the French Institute. In 1948 we received our naturalization papers – I clearly remember the excitement that day in our home. Despite my father's age (he was over 40 years old), he was conscripted to the British army and served in the Pioneer Corps. His call-up left my mother to cope alone with five young children in a foreign country. Although she spoke fluent German, French, Italian and Yiddish, she had no knowledge of English and had no close friends or family.

After the war ended my father worked by day (and often by night) to support our family. He worked in hotels while at the same time he gradually built up his own credit drapery business. My mother was very occupied with bringing up five young children, but also gave language lessons in French, German and Italian to teachers at my primary school. These pupils became her friends.

My parents set about establishing themselves within the Torquay and Paignton Hebrew Congregation. During and immediately after the war there was an influx of Jews (mainly Sephardim) from London and it was a warm and flourishing community. They were particularly supportive when my elder brother Henry celebrated his Bar-Mitzvah. Gradually these Jews returned to their homes in London and when the community became too small to support a Rabbi, my father took on the role of lay-leader and minister at Synagogue services until he retired and my parents moved to Bournemouth in 1970. As for me, I married my husband Gerry Moss in 1959 and we lived in London with our two children Steven and Nicky.

At the age of 19 Nicky went to a kibbutz in Israel for a year of voluntary work under the auspices of Sh'nat Sherut. Here she met her future husband Moshe and she decided she wanted to spend her life in Israel. They were married in 1985 and have three children, Danielle, aged 20 years (now serving in the Israeli army), Adam, aged 17 (shortly to serve in the Israeli army) and Maya, aged 12. Nicky runs the baby nursery on the kibbutz. Steven studied medicine, married Lisa in 1986 and immigrated to USA where he is now professor of gastroenterology at Rhode Island hospital. They have two children, Jacob aged 8 and Tasha aged 6. Needless to say our five grandchildren continue to give us great pleasure. Last year (2006) Gerry and I decided to make Aliyah and now live in Netanya in Israel.

While we were growing up, my parents spoke very little of the hardships they had endured during those troubled years. They realized how fortunate they had been to have survived, given the fate of so many of their friends and family. My father's eldest sister was in a concentration camp but survived and it was not until such time as he went to France to meet her in 1951 and saw the numbers on her arm that he started to speak to us about life in Nazi Germany.

We were indeed blessed and with each passing year I realize ever more the extent of our good fortune in having escaped Nazi Germany as a complete family.

✡ ✡ ✡

Elisabeth and Lux Adorno pose for a good-bye portrait on the streets of Frankfort, Germany. (Courtesy USHMM)

CHAPTER 5: A SAD TALE OF MISSED CHANCES

Manfred Alweiss arrived in England on September 1, 1939. He embarked on a dangerous journey out of Berlin and into Harwich, England at the cusp of the war. The Kindertransport journey was forced to cease its operation entirely due to the outbreak of war in England; therefore, Manfred and the other refugees were the last to be rescued. Thankfully, a gracious

Dutch woman assisted with transportation by bus because no more trains were permitted to cross into Holland. They arrived in England just in the knick of time. Manfred's sister was also supposed to be on the transport, but due to the shortage of seats and the approaching disaster (the Germans), her name, along with many others, was taken off the list. Manfred recalls his trip as a "political crisis."

His mother had the chance to flee to London and work as a domestic, but she refused to be a maid. Sadly, that decision was a mistake and she, along with her daughter, were later killed by the Nazis. Manfred states, "I regret that my mother did not have the foresight to flee to London when the opportunity arrived. However, at the time hardly anyone expected what was going on."

After a night train journey from Berlin to Cologne, Germany, the train journey had to end because all the rail traffic had been stopped across the frontier because of the political crisis. We were then bussed across the frontier to Hoek van Holland, organized by a courageous Dutch lady from the Dutch refugee committee, we were greeted by the news that Germany had invaded Poland that morning: the beginning of World War Two.

We arrived in Cologne the next morning and were told that the frontier had been closed and no more trains would be allowed to cross into Holland. The Jewish community put us up in a Jewish youth hotel, where we spent a further anxious night, wondering whether we would be turned back. However, to our immense relief, two buses arrived from Holland the next morning, to

5: A Sad Tale of Missed Chances

drive us across the frontier and then to the Hook. We learned much later, that these buses had been organized by a courageous lad (a gentile) from the Dutch refugee committee. She personally took charge of us. When we reached the frontier we were confronted by a frontier guard who stood, somewhat dramatically, in the middle of the road, with his rifle raised as if he was about to fire at us. Our plucky lady protector got out and showed our transit papers to the guard. After some consultation, he waved us through, shouting, "Judenkinder" (Jew kids) to his comrades. I will never forget the immense felling of relief which swept through the bus the moment we crossed the border. This lady was later honored as a "righteous Gentile" at Yad Vashem.

During the train journey to Liverpool Street, I was surprised by the comfortable upholstered seats (not known in pre-war Germany third class compartments) and disgusted by the tea we were served which I spat out immediately thinking it was coffee. I only knew tea without milk and with lemon. When we arrived at Liverpool Street Station, it was crowded with evacuees and soldiers putting up sandbags. We were told that we would immediately proceed to a holding camp in Wales. This was Gwrych Castle, in Abergele in North Wales. I and the other secular chaverim (friends) were later sorted out and sent to another castle in South Wales. In spite of the primitive accommodations at Gwrych, I retain a pleasant memory of our Madrich (leader) Erwin Seligman. He took a personal caring interest in us all, whether orthodox or not. Although I later became disillusioned with the prospect of becoming a Chalutz, I retain fond memories of the senses of fellowship and mission which imbued us.

My father left Germany for Paris when Hitler became chancellor in 1933 and in 1936 my mother joined him. Soon after they both left for Palestine and we were to join them however, my mother was disappointed by the conditions in Palestine in those days and decided to return to Germany, where she was sure, life would, in the long run, be more tolerable. After Kristallnacht she, together with most other Jews in Germany saw their mistake. Mother then decided to join my father who had moved to London by then. However, mom refused to take a job as a domestic servant in England, which was the only way she would receive a UK visa.

So she just applied for my sister and me to join the Kindertransport. By the time we were put on the list, it was August 1939, we were informed that a transport would leave but only a small number of children could go (reduced amount). I was put on the list, but regrettably my sister was dropped. A few months later my mother and sister managed to cross the border of Belgium on foot, guided by a smuggler. They settled in Antwerp, only to join the flood of refugees in May of 1940, fleeing from the invading German army. When they reached La Panne at the boarder of France they were overtaken by the German army, who ordered all refugees to return to their respective towns of residence. By 1943 they moved to Brussels and hid with a Belgium family. Unfortunately, they decided to briefly return to their previous residence where they were caught by the

5: A Sad Tale of Missed Chances

German police and sent to Malines, the transit camp to Auschwitz where they were both gassed on arrival.

All this could have been envisioned by me, or by any of my fellow Kinder, when we bade farewell to our loved ones on that evening in Berlin. When we arrived at the station we were allocated, much to our surprise, seats in comfortable compartments. This was all the more surprising because the gangways were packed with German army personnel who had to stand (for a long journey) and who were being mobilized for the conflict which their leadership had evidently already planned. After a while the door of our compartment was opened by a German Army officer who asked, very politely, whether there was a vacant seat, which we affirmed with some trepidation. We soon got talking to him and he turned out to be a sympathetic person. He expressed his great regret that we were made to flee. After this, on this long night journey to Cologne, I fell asleep on his shoulder! A pleasant memory of my last personal contact with a German before the war.

Manfred married and had two beautiful children. He was a chartered accountant for many years then a partner for Price Waterhouse. Currently, Manfred is retired, a member of the Kindertransport Association, and a devoted grandfather.

CHAPTER 6: SEPARATED FROM MY PARENTS FOR HALF MY LIFE

Ellen Bottner was born in 1933 in the Black Forest Region of Germany, Rexingen. Her older sister, Inge Bottner, was born in 1930, and the two shared a tight bond. They were surrounded by a large, loving family and thrived. This ended when the Germans raged a fierce war against the Jews. In July of 1939, Ellen and her sister traveled on the Kindertransport and had no idea if they would ever see their parents again. They were only six and nine, but somehow their parents had the will to send their sweet babies away.

Ellen shares her thoughts about her desire to educate future generations about the perils of war and hatred, "It is my intention to share with others, less familiar with the turbulent years before World War II in Europe, so that they too may gain an understanding of the disruption and tragedies that affected many families, separating innocent children from their parents and affecting their family life in both positive and sad ways."

I remember clearly Kristallnacht on November 9, 1938. I was only five years old but the trauma of that night is still clear in my mind. The German soldiers came to our house looking for Jewish men. My father had to hide in a horse feeding trough to escape the torment. Soon after that my father had to work for the Germans, giving up his own cattle dealer business. My father went to work every day using Inge's bicycle. I remember the hysteria one day when the bike was broken and there was no other means of transportation to get my father to work. I also recall the intense fear of the German soldiers as they goose stepped through town while our parents held us tightly.

My memory of my departure from Germany is still hazy. I do remember, on a warm day in early July, 1939, being bundled up by my mother in many layers of clothing (including a winter coat). Inge and I boarded the train with my mother. It must have been wrenching for my mother to put us on a boat to England, not knowing when or if we would be reunited and who might take care of her two young girls. We were six and nine years old respectively. We were sleeping in the lower bunk in a ship's cabin, together with many other children. The next morning we had breakfast in the ship's dining room, where we were served fruit and white bread, which we had never see before. We thought we were eating cake.

We arrived in England on July 7, 1939. We took the train to London and meet my mother's sister, aunt Lisa (who had immigrated to England earlier and worked as a maid). We then took a train to Manchester, England where we were to live with Willie and Ray Shalyt. Thus starting a new chapter in our lives as two English/British girls.

The new lifestyle we were about to enter was suggested by the chauffeur who picked us up at the Manchester railroad station to transport us to the Shalyt's home, called Easthome, in Preswich. I was particularly impressed by the beautiful manicured lawns, the blooming

6: Separated From My Parents For Half My Life

flowers and the magnificent home which was soon to be our temporary home. The house belonged to Uncle Willie, as we called our British host, and his wife Ray. He was a Russian, Jewish immigrant who owned a successful linen business. The house had central heat, a novelty for us, and sported a dog, an Irish Setter named Rufus. The Shalyts had two daughters, Cecil and Paulina, both older than me. We were treated royally and lived better than we did in Germany. In September after just one summer in Manchester, Inge and I started school in England. Upon arrival in England, neither Inge nor I understood a word of English. However, as young girls we learned the language quickly since there were no other German speaking adults or children with whom we had a daily relationship.

Our new, peaceful life with the Shalyt's was interrupted by World War II and the German bombing of England. One day in the fall of 1939, after just a few weeks in the local school, Uncle Willie took us to school with suitcases. I remember standing around and meeting Maria and Adele Dunn, local school girls, whose father was a friend of Uncle Willie. All the children in town were being evacuated to a rural location, much less likely to be bombed by the Germans. Since Inga and I spoke very little English, Marie (who was the oldest) was told not to let us out of her sight and, no matter what happens, not to go anywhere without us. We boarded the train and headed to Fleetwood (a small fishing village). I remember standing in the town hall, milling around while the townspeople selected their new charges. Into our lives came Maude and Murial Bailey! The two sisters, like many other town folks, volunteered to take city children into their homes. They signed up for two children but [ended] up with the four of us: Marie, Adele, Inge and Ellen. Thank goodness their home was big enough to accommodate all of us. Their father was a prominent figure in town and even had the high school named after him. Attached to the Bailey residence was a school building, once run by Aunt Maude. The school was now closed because the army had taken it over. Aunt Muriel was the principal of the local elementary school. Again we were very well taken care of kindly Angelican ladies, who even helped us keep up our Jewish identity. A rabbi came to town every few weeks to help us celebrate Jewish festivals so we would not forget our religious customs. On all of the Jewish high holidays, we returned to Manchester to stay with the Shalyts. One Passover, American Soldiers (including a chaplain) came to our house for Passover. One of the soldiers was from New York. He wrote his wife about us and she, in turn, got in touch with our parents (who escaped Germany and made their way to the US). It must have been comforting to my parents to receive independent confirmation of our well being.

Sometime in 1940 Uncle Willie took us to London so we could get American Passports for eventual immigration to the United States. We stayed, with Uncle Willie's relative and there experienced our first real encounter with the horror of war. I remember sleeping in the air raid shelter of the relative's home. The next day we went to the American Embassy to get our papers. Shortly after leaving the embassy the air raid sirens went off and we ran to Victoria Station to catch our train bound for Manchester. Search lights streaked the skies and guns were blasting away. Most people fell to the ground. We rushed onto a train which hightailed it out of London. We arrived in Manchester safely but the sound of sirens still ringing in our ears.

Between Manchester and Fleetwood we led a good life and lacked for no material objects. As an adult, looking back at those days, I realize that there was no one for me but my sister Inge to give love and comfort to a little girl. My sister, of course, needed the same. But at that age, this is what I thought was a normal life and did not feel deprived. The deprivation happened much later. We had many advantages that would have been lacking had we stayed with our parents in a peaceful, rural German village. While in England, Inge and I were very well educated, lived in a cultured home with access to theatres, music, and books. We even received piano lessons! We were taught English manners and developed some distinctively British attitudes that are likely still with me today. We learned to enjoy and appreciate the better things in life.

In the summer of 1944 Marie and Adele returned to Manchester and their family. Inge and I also left Fleetwood and went to live in a hostel in Blackpool with other German Jewish children refugees, referred to as "kinder," German for children. The hostel was supported by the local Jewish community. Most of the girls had no knowledge of the whereabouts of their parents and were very jealous of Inge and me, since we did know that our parents were safe in the United States. The jealousy of the children in the hostel flared up regularly, every time we received a letter of package from our parents. Every time a candy-ladden parcel arrived, a fight broke out. Even out head mistress thought it should be shared with everyone in the house, and we thought it belonged to us. This was not a happy time since communial living was alien to us.

We went to Fleetwood quite often to visit Aunt Maud and Muriel, or to sleep over weekends. Just before the Christmas holidays in 1944 we packed up all our belongings and went back to Manchester. We were told we would be leaving for the United States. Weeks passed and nothing happened. We returned to Blackpool and school. We could not talk about our awaited trip since "walls have ears" and "loose lips can sink ships" as I learned later.

In February 1945 we again quickly packed our bags and headed back to Manchester. We were there for just a few days. Uncle Willie took us to Liverpool to board a Danish cargo ship called the M.S. Eria. In addition to cargo, the ship carried about 50 passengers, mostly German Jews, and we were the youngest aboard. Inge and I had a beautiful cabin on the main deck. We were put in charge of a young lady whose name I don't recall who [was] bound for Buffalo, N.Y. Being young we did not recognize the multiple dangers of crossing the Atlantic in wartime: First, and deadliest were the German submarines or U-boat, as they were then known. The second hazard was the stormy Atlantic weather. We fortunately escaped the former but were soon made miserable by the latter. To discourage U-Boat attacks, our ship traveled in a huge convoy. There were ships as far as you could see.

On the more upbeat side there was the food. After years of living on rations of one egg a week, we were ready to pig out. The first night aboard ship we went to the dining room and saw the most lavish buffet spread we had ever seen in our lives so pig out we did! That was my first and last enjoyable meal aboard ship. The next morning, as we steamed out of Liverpool, I immediately became seasick and I stayed that way until we docked. I spent every day on the deck, hanging over the rail, with everyone trying to comfort me. I got lots of attention because I was the youngest passenger aboard. Each night I returned to our cabin and lay on my bed right next to the bucket wedged in between Inge's and my bed.

An interesting coincidence took place aboard our ship. Among the passengers on the M.S. Eria was a German lady named Lily Brill, bound for New York to be with her married daughter, Irma Waller. We soon learned that Lily Brill was also a relative of mine: Her daughter, Ruth (Liselotte) Brill, went to Israel (actually Palestine at the time) and married my Uncle Seligman (Pinchas) Levi. I finally got to meet Uncle Sele and Ruth Levi 11 years later, when they also immigrated to the United States in 1956.

After two weeks seasickness we finally spotted land it was Halifax, Nova Scotia. That evening was my second trip to the dining room but to no avail: I just couldn't stand the sight of food. To this day you won't find me on a cruise ship! The next day we debarked in Halifax, our papers were checked and we boarded a train from Nova

Scotia headed for New York City. Our parents awaited us anxiously.

While Inga and I were in England, my parents were also fortunate enough to leave Germany. My father left the very day war broke out, September 1, 1939. My mother left even later, in May of 1941, on one of the last ships to leave Holland before it too fell to the Germans. Both parents came straight to America. I mentioned earlier that while Inga and I were still in England, we received our passports with permission to come to the U.S.A. Our mother was originally planning to pick us up in England, enroute to the United States. By the time she made the passage, children were no longer allowed to leave England. The Germans had recently torpedoed a ship in the Atlantic full of British children being sent to Canada for the duration of the war. All the passengers were lost. As a result our parents lost the opportunity for an early reunion with their daughters. By the time of our upcoming reunion at Penn station we had been separated for almost six years about half my life time at the time.

Pennsylvania Station, in the heart of New York City was a site of great joy that day in February of 1945. Tears came to our eyes too when we arrived. At first I didn't recognize my father but my mother looked the same. The joyful reunion turned to consternation as we boarded the noisy New York Subway on our way to Washington Heights. Many German Jews, recently arrived in the U.S, settled in that uptown Manhattan neighborhood. Our dreams of living in the United States disintegrated completely as we entered our new home. My parents lived in a dilapidated apartment building, in a sparsely furnished four room apartment with crumbling walls and a musty smell. We immediately longed for our homes in England where we lived in a private home, surrounded by lavish gardens.

We resisted the cultural adjustments we had to make from a well-to-do British style of living to a relatively poor, strict disciplined German model of a family. Everything about the German culture was different: food was overcooked, culture, books, the arts were all absent and economic survival was foremost on my parents mind. They believed that life centered on work, economic survival and the necessities of eating and sleeping. Money was not to be spent on anything but the necessities. Even baths were to be taken only once a week and coordinated with our weekly change of clothes. At our parent's insistence, we wore the same clothes all week long. We were young teenagers then, 13 and 16 years old, and could never go back to the strict German way of life we knew as young children. The disappointment must have been equally difficult for my parents. They expected two little girls, unchanged by the last six years, who would be completely obedient and as comfortable with the German way of little now as they were six years earlier. They got instead two disappointed teens who dreamed of a different life, filled with luxuries, love and devotion. Our disappointment with each other led to alienation between parents and daughters. Unfortunately, this state was never rectified.

Ellen and Inga Bottner often dreamed about visiting England, and in 1976 after a long awaited reunion with the people who treated them with love and kindness, their wish came true. Ellen describes the reunion as "Happy" and that it "surpassed their expectations." Ellen wished that her relationship with her parents had not been so strained, and she has some regrets. "I wished that I discussed with my parents the emotions felt upon departure, the reunion and the disappointments." Unfortunately, the girls never articulated their anguish, fears, and letdowns to their parents. Perhaps, if they had, it would have rekindled a relationship amidst their tumultuous existence.

Ilse Lichtenstein on the steps outside a children's home. (Courtesy USHMM)

CHAPTER 7: TORN APART

The Lichtenstein family hoped for the day when freedom would be at their doorstep and the American dream within their reach. They desired to escape from the soaring violence and anti-Semitism that had plagued Germany in the 1930s. To protect their young children from the pending war, they sent Inga and Ilse on the Kindertransport. They left on January 4, 1939, traveled approximately 350 miles, and embarked on a new life in the Netherlands. Sixteen months after their arrival, war broke out in the Netherlands and Inga's foster family shipped her back to Germany. As fate would have it, Inga met her death at the hands of the Nazis along with some of her family. Their dream to live in the United States as an intact family, sadly, never came true.

My family (Meinhard and Kaethe Lichtenstein) lived in the remote town of Volkmarsen, Germany. We were a middle class family who operated a successful tailoring business from our residence. We worked hard and enjoyed the comforts of an upper class life style. On May 7, 1920, our family was blessed with a little baby boy who we named Arthur, three years later I (Ilse) was born on February 24, 1923 the youngest child Inge arrived on February 4, 1930. We attended regular public school growing up, but also received formal Jewish education weekly.

By January of 1939; our once intact family was completely separated throughout the world in an attempt to evade the dangerous times for Jews. My brother Arthur left Germany at age eighteen to immigrate to the United States. My sister and I (Ilse and Inga) left on the Kindertransport on January 4, 1939, where we embarked on an exhausting twelve hour trip to the Netherlands. Our parents remained in Germany hoping that our entire family would immigrate to America someday. Out of desperation, they send us out of the country to evade the tragedies of war and shield our young spirits from the wickedness that soon erupted.

I was the oldest refugee (age 16) amongst the transports therefore; I graciously cared for the younger

7: Torn Apart

children as my motherly instincts materialized on the voyage. Inga was only nine years old during the trip and simply hoped for a speedy reunion with our parents. For eighteen months my sister and I remained together while living in numerous homes, but on September of 1939 Inge was accepted to live with a Jewish family in Blydorp. In the interim, Arthur tried to secure admittance to the United States for the entire family but he only succeeded in sending me. The news was bittersweet. On April 4, 1940 after living in the Netherlands for 16 months I said good-bye to my sister and boarded the Volendam to New York where I felt fortunate yet befuddled by the separation. Remarkably I occupied the last remaining seat on the ship. On April 16th I woke up at 4:00 a.m. to see the Statue of Liberty. I was then detained on the ship upon arrival until my brother from Wisconsin came up with the $100 that was due for the voyage. Unfortunately, my parents continued to remain in Germany and the Nazis were raging a war against Jews that made it impossible to escape.

In May of 1940 Germany invaded the Netherlands therefore; Inga's foster family shipped her back to Germany to live with our parents in order to avoid the soaring violence. The move changed the course of her life forever because the vile anti-Semitism was so rampant that their lives were in danger. Sadly, on June 1, 1942 Meinhard, Kaethe and Inga were sent to Sobibor and wretchedly murdered. The news was so disheartening.

I remained in the United States along with my older brother Arthur. We lost our parents, sister and home but we still had the love and support of one another.

Eventually we began to settle in to our new lives in America. I reunited with a childhood friend who also immigrated from Germany, Meinhard Meyer. We became close friends and were a true comfort to one another. Meinhard's sister, Berthe was also part of the Kindertransport and coincidentally she and I lived in the same children's home together. Berthe along with her parents were set to leave Holland on May 7, 1940 and reside in the United States along with their son. On the night before they were set to sail, Germany invaded Holland and they were trapped, the news was dreadful and the family was terrified. On May 28, 1943 Berthe and her parents were murdered in Sobibor and their dreams were lost forever.

Meinhard Meyer was drafted in the American Army one month after his family's death. He was sent to the Pacific theater. In February of 1945 after serving for almost two years, he came home, reunited with me and we married in 1955. Meinhard and I shared the same grief; our parents and siblings were murdered by the Nazis but the memory of them will forever be imprinted in our hearts.

Meinhard and Ilse are happily married and still live in America. Ilse worked as a maid in a knitting factory then moved to Cleveland, Ohio and received a job in a meatpacking plant. She enrolled in beauty school while working at the plant at night. Ilse attends many speaking engagements where she graciously shares her Holocaust story. Looking back, she

7: Torn Apart

recalls when her family wrote to the American Consulate to receive their number for a visa, "Only 20,000 visas were given out, mine was 16,540." Several weeks later, her parents tried to obtain their number, but it was 24,460. Sadly, their lives ended before they could make it out of Germany.

CHAPTER 8: CONTINUOUS DISARRAY

Franz and Helene had three children: Agathe, born on July 8, 1930; Elizabeth, born on December 2, 1925; and the youngest, Lux, a baby boy born on June 23, 1927. They resided in Eschersheim, Germany, a district of Frankfurt. Helene descended from a prosperous family in Luebeck and studied music at the renounced Hoch'sche Conservatory. Her father was a well-known historian. This is the story of Elizabeth.

In 1917 my mother, Helen met her future husband Franz while studying law and violin at the Conservatory. My dad came from a French military family and my grandmother was Jewish while my grandfather was half-Jewish. We observed the Christian faith. In 1929 dad received a position as a Judge therefore, we moved to Dortmund, Germany. By 1933 the Nazi regime took root and on April 29, 1933 dad was fired because he was part Jewish. We lost the security of his position therefore, we moved back to Eschersheim, Germany to reestablish ourselves.

My dad was hired by The Jewish Cultural Council Orchestra as a music teacher. Due to the Nuremberg Laws of the time he was only permitted to teach non-Aryans. (Jews, half-Jews gypsies, and anyone described by the law as non-Aryan). To his astonishment, several years later his teaching position was revoked because the Council only wanted Jews that descended from two Jewish parents and Franz was only half-Jewish. He was stuck between a rock and a hard place as he was being persecuted on both fronts; from the Jews and the Aryans. We moved once again in 1935 to Frankfort, Germany where dad played in ensembles and provided lectures for a living.

From 1936–1938 our family began seeking ways out of Germany since our opportunities were narrowing and persecution was soaring. In December of 1938 we learned that the waiting time to immigrate to the United States was approximately 36 months; the news was alarming. Instead, my parents decided to send the children to England and seek salvation for themselves at a later time. Initially, two of us were sent on the Kindertransport; myself (Elizabeth) and Lux. We arrived on June 27, 1939 and were met by Mr. and Mrs. Hulford (a nephew of the families' dentist from Germany). Soon after our arrival the war broke out in England and the Hulford's could no longer care for us. Unfortunately, we were separated and Lux went to a hostel for boys while I went to another home. After several months, we met up with our fathers' previous piano teacher Mrs. Goldstein from Germany but our stay was short lived because the town was soon evacuated due to the looming war. Ultimately I settled with Mrs. Heyes a gracious woman who was caring and loving. I lived in her home for a decade; thrived in her care and by 1941 earned my school certificate then proceeded onto business school. I continued my catholic education and was confirmed at the Watford Parish Church. Lux came to live with Mrs. Heyes as well and earned his school certificate. The predictability

8: Continuous Disarray

of our stable home brought comfort to us therefore, we were progressing nicely.

In the interim my parents moved from Frankfurt to Zwingenberg to avoid the soaring violence. By 1943, my dad was distraught when he learned that he was registered for a labor camp; so he went into hiding with friends but eventually hid at the Buehler Hoehe (a sanatorium). He successfully evaded the Nazis and longed to be reunited with his dear family. Luz and I finally received word that our parents and sister, Agathe were alright and a reunion was arranged. We saw them for the very first time after an eight year separation and were delighted that every one was safe. Then in 1948 three years after the war ended Lux and I visited our family back in Germany once again, rekindled our relationship and forever cherished the fact that somehow we all survived the war.

Elizabeth remained in England, became a British citizen, and married in 1950. Franz became a judge in 1949 and then was named President of the Senate in Frankfort, Germany.

CHAPTER 9: TORMENTED ON THE STREETS OF MUNICH

Micheal and Mathilde married and had two beautiful children: Hans and Marie. They were a prominent upper-class family. Micheal was a well-known attorney and an active member of the community while Mathilde was an avid artist. On March 10, 1933, storm troopers beat their father at police headquarters and used him as a means to send a message to the whole community: don't complain! He was then forced to march throughout the streets barefoot, and injured from the beating. The violence Michael endured on the streets of Munich was an atrocity and a testament to the severe persecution that occurred early during Hitler's reign. It was apparent that justice was no longer a God-given right for the Jews. This is Maria's story.

Two months after Adolf Hitler was named chancellor of Germany, storm troopers violently beat my dad leaving him bruised, bleeding and completely humiliated! With his trousers cut off at the knees and left barefoot they proceeded to torment him by parading him up and down the streets of Munich with a sign draped from his neck that read, "I am a Jew, but I will never complain to the police." The unfortunate stunt was perpetrated because earlier that morning on March 10, 1933, dad was informing police about his client Max Uhlfelder. Max's downtown store was vandalized by the SA; he was arrested and sent to the Dachau concentration camp. The anti-Semitism was prolific and sadly both men were tormented.

I was home ill from school at the time, and witnessed my father's deplorable condition; he was drenched in blood and visibly shaken. The scene devastated me terribly as I was only eight years old and did not understand why someone would harm my good natured father. I then transferred from the local public school and was sent to a Jewish school. Then in 1935 I attended St. Anna Lyzeum School for three years. Simultaneously, the persecution continued to haunt the community. After Krystallnacht on November 9, 1938 I transferred once more, to a Jewish vocational school where I studied restaurant management.

By March of 1939 Hans (my brother) was determined to leave Munich behind; he received a job in England then joined the British army. Subsequently, I was placed on the Kindertansport list and in June 1939, at the tender age of fourteen, I left for England. I was greeted by Mrs. Williams a gracious woman who took me in and another child as well. While I was adjusting to my new life in England sadly, Mrs. Williams died abruptly in 1940. Myself and the other refugee were offered housing with Mrs. Williams's son, Colonel Ainslie Williams and his wife Hilda. Mrs. Williams graciously left a trust fund for us for our future education; her generosity was greatly appreciated. In 1942 I furthered my studies and enrolled in the local University.

My father vehemently tried to obtain American visas for the family but the immigration quotas filled quickly and he was not successful. Instead, he decided to flee to South America initially, he studied Spanish to prepare for his hopeful departure. He hired a Spanish tutor,

9: Tormented on The Streets of Munich

a student from Peru who was financially depleted and therefore trapped in Munich himself. My father sympathized with his dilemma and offered to pay for his tutoring sessions in advance. They established a close friendship and the tutor appreciated his gracious offering. Through their conversations the tutor learned that dad was aspiring to leave Munich for South America in an effort to flee from the persecution. The tutor's father happened to be the Minister of the interior in Peru. Within weeks he ensured visas for my parents in an effort to save their lives. After a long exhausting trip my parents arrived in Peru on November 1940. Dad quickly settled into his new life and his past became a painful but distant memory.

Michael became President of the German Jewish Refugee Committee and assisted families with compensation payments. The man once tormented on the streets of Munich was then free to help his fellow sufferers.

CHAPTER 10: THEY DIED - I SURVIVED!

Alfred Terry was a rambunctious and insightful young boy who managed to secure his own passport at the tender age of 11. He even wore a swastika to disguise himself as a gentile in order to purchase food for the family while maneuvering on the streets of Vienna on his bicycle. This remarkable boy arrived on the Kindertransport in January of 1939. For two years, a loving Christian brotherhood community in Wiltshire cared for him. By 1942, his parents were forcibly thrown into a cattle car and left to suffer a hellish ride. Upon arrival in Minsk, they along with many others were murdered. The death of his parents by the Nazis was devastating. "Having now reached over 75 years, I wonder if, as a child, I could have done anything to persuade my parents to try to save themselves." Unfortunately, the millions of suffering victims could not foresee their eminent danger. The end was simply incomprehensible.

My mother was the finest, kindest person you can imagine. As a child I was very lucky! In my old age I'm thinking deeper, it seems; maybe it will help my sanity. Little did I realize on that faithful night when I said good-byes at the concourse of the Wiener Westbahnhof that I'd never see my poor parent's again! All I knew was that new visas were before me, when as an eleven-year-old boy I caught the Kindertransport in mid-January 1939 from Vienna. I was an only child, very likely spoiled, and now I was on my way to England.

After having spent months in 1938 running around quite alone from one government office to the other in Vienna, so that I could also go and apply for my passport at the end, arriving at the Prinz Strasse in the snow at an unearthly hour in the morning, I experienced a miracle which made it possible for me to get into the building in mid-morning (without quivering for a week or longer with all the others who stood outside shivering), run up the staircase and get past every one of the 21 examining tables, and successfully get my passport application completed! Later I returned to collect this document, a linen-bound book which bears my photo. My mother was amazed that I'd managed it, neither she nor Frau Professor Tedesco, for whom she was cleaning to get enough for us to eat, could believe what I, an 11-year-old, had achieved.

Our small sweetshop had been stolen from us after the Anschluss, and my father was barred from teaching his 'students'. He, now suffering a massive nervous breakdown, which completely incapacitated him! I devoured the wonderful books of Frau Professor Tedesco's extensive library in any spare moment; her flat was near ours at the Nussdorferstr/Alserbachstr Junction, I think it was in the Sechssch Gasse. I wonder what became of that kind, nice lady. Our own small flat was No. 73 Liechtensteinstrasse, door 5. That was just around the corner from the Alserbachstrasse, where, in the Markthalle I often went to buy a little food as I looked the least Jewish of our family, and surreptitiously used my chromium swastika, the wearing of which became necessary to do any sort of shopping. My bicycle took me

10: They Died - I Survived!

all over the city to get my various papers during that autumn. The restrictions on cycling had been lifted for children (in fact I had a permit from the police for which I had passed the test). Under Hitler and Vienna traffic had all changed from left to right as in the Reich. We had Schllings and marks and for a time could use either!

Well, my Kindertransport train sped through the night, and when we neared the German/Dutch frontier the Nazis came and frightened all the children by shouting that if anyone was caught with valuables in the coming search the entire train would be returned to Vienna. There was a lot of crying from the children, but we rolled over the frontier without any kind of search at all. I could have carried anything. Finally, after a few more adventures I reached my destination in Wiltshire, on a huge farm, the Bruderhof! It was near Ashton Keynes, not far from Swindon. I was looked after very well, but in a simple fashion, at this religious Christian brotherhood community until January 1942, that is exactly 2 years.

While I was safe in England, my poor parents were shunted around various unsatisfactory addresses in Vienna and somehow survived until 22 September 1942. The last address was Vienna II, Raimundgasse 4/4. Of course I never knew that at the time. Early in the morning of 22 September 1942 they were rudely woken and made to sign the Vermogens-Verzeichnis (which was a declaration of any money they possessed! Of course they had none!) and forced like cattle into trucks at a goods station, without food or water on the long journey to Minsk. It was the last fateful trip of their haunted lives, where many thousands of others had gone before them and others followed to their deaths on arrival near Minsk. These death trains were re-commenced soon after the Wannsee Conference in Germany, where Reinhard Heydrich was prominent and Hitler's Final Solution for the Jews was plotted. On 6 May 1942 a deportation train with over 990 Jewish men, women and children left the Vienna Aspang rail station for Minsk. The executions were carried out a few Km from Maly Trostinec, a former Communist farming commune, in the pine forests, where pits were ready dug for their arrival. Later, when gas was available, the murders were carried out in the wagons. Before I received this detailed report, I'd never even heard of Maly Trostinec, and hardly anybody I have spoken to had either! Dozens of regular trainloads followed in 1942 and all the Jews who were still in Vienna became victims. I think it was about 90,000 who went to Minsk that year, some also from other cities in Europe!

There are no records of any survivors; everything seems to have been hushed up until now. The previous reports I received 30 or 40 years ago from officialdom in Vienna, I am now able to form a picture of the truth, and this has made me doubly sad and caused me sleepless nights once again.

Sadly, Alfred Terry died in June of 2006. He leaves one son, two daughters, and his lovely wife whom he was married to for 53 years.

✵ ✵ ✵

CHAPTER 11: THANKFUL TO BE SAFE

Julius Fleischer (now Fletcher) can trace his ancestry back to the 1690's when his family originated in southern Germany. Julius was the last male in his Jewish family. His father managed a prosperous jewelry company and they lived an affluent lifestyle in Frankfort, Germany. By the time of Hitler's reign, the once well-to-do family was penniless due to the many restrictions placed on them. Julius left on the Kindertransport under remarkable conditions. He was 18 while the age limit was 16. Julius along with 34 others defied the odds and somehow managed to flee despite the rules. He describes his unique situation, "I would like to write about a group of boys and girls never mentioned in any report dealing with the Kindertransport." Fortunately, the rules were bent and the children joined the exodus.

Officially the upper age limit for the transport was 16 but I, like many others, was almost 18 years old well above the limit when we arrived in London as part of the Kindertransport. I was the eldest of 12 boys from the Anlernwerkstatt the Jewish technical school in Frankfort to come to London. After Kristallnacht anyone over age 16 was deported and sent to a concentration camp. I convinced the guard that I was younger and the plan worked.

My father was an involved Social Democrat. One day her left the house to visit a friend but never returned. His body was later recovered in a near-by river and it was deemed a suicide by drowning. However, no water was ever found in his lungs. I had to identify his body since my mother was simply to torn apart to do so.

After the disaster of the Kristallnacht our dedicated head Mr. Bernhard Beling, a Christian, got in touch with the German Jewish Aid Committee at Bloomsbury House to help us, in most cases penniless, to leave Germany. As minors we needed an arrangement from our parents that they were prepared to let us leave the country. My mother agreed to let me leave Frankfort as a member of the Kindertransport, destination London.

A total of 34 students were rescued before the 3 September 1939 all members of the Kindertransport and all over 16. It was the first time that we had left Germany, supported by a limited knowledge of school English.

First stop of the journey was Amsterdam, where we were welcomed at a big reception organization by the local Jewish community, then via hook of Holland by boat to Harwich, eventually arriving on the 4 May 1939 in the afternoon at Liverpool Street Station. All the children were met by their sponsors but our group was two hours later still waiting without supervision for someone to meet us. After a phone call to Bloomsbury House we were told that they were very sorry they got their date mixed up, but would soon meet us and take the group to a very nice hotel. One hour later we walked to our hotel, the Jews' Temporary Schelter in Mansell Street. So almost four hours late we arrived at the shelter to be told you are too late it's full. We shall take you to a nice hotel around the corner. We were taken to the Rowton House, a doss house in Mile End Road.

11: Thankful to be Safe

This was our introduction to London. But in the end they did find us a very nice hostel as a temporary accommodation. I would just like to show how difficult it was for some youth to settle in a new country without real support. There must have been others with similar experiences, thankful to be in England and thankful to be safe. As far as I have discovered only one other ex-member of the Anlernwerkstatt of 34 saved is still alive today. I later found out that my mother was killed in Kovno and other members of my family who lived in Southern Germany, Stasbourg were killed in Auschwitz.

Julius possessed a flair for art and desired to become a sculptor, but the war interrupted his plans. Instead, he was an engineer for over 20 years then worked for the British Airways. After sharing his insightful story, he died. He and the other 34 Kindertransport refugees who fled from Nazi territory in September of 1939 have all passed away.

✯ ✯ ✯

CHAPTER 12: THE DIARY OF DIRK

Dirk and Keetje Heide grew up in a wealthy Dutch household in Rotterdam, Holland. Their father was a veterinarian and their mother was head of the children's ward at a local hospital. Dirk Heide (age 12) and his younger sister Keetje (age 9) made a dramatic escape to England while the Germans were advancing into Holland. Their departure was documented in Dirk's diary, which outlines the war in Holland, his mother's tragic death by Luftwaffe bombs, and the Blitz in London. The diary concludes with the children leaving England and embarking on a children's ship to America while dodging U-boats along the way. They were escorted to England by their Uncle Pieter, a World War I Veteran who despised the Nazis and referred to them as, "damned swine." While serving in the First World War, four of his fingers were severed; the devastation only fueled his hatred for the Germans. Uncle Pieter was not permitted to go to America with the children due to the restrictions placed on him, and he had to return to Holland. Once in America, Dirk and Keetje were met by their Aunt and Uncle, Mr. and Mrs. Klass. The passages outlined below reveal a portion of his diary-their voyage to England then America. Dirk, at an age of innocence, clearly articulates the sacrifice and suffering of his family. The excessive bombing and loss of his mother had an everlasting effect on him. To protect their identities, all of the names in the diary have been changed.

The 10,000 Children That Hitler Missed

Wednesday May 15, 1940

We have been in England all morning. It was daylight almost when our boat got in. We landed at a place called Harwich. Everyone cheered and sang when we came into the harbor safely. We took the train to London, which took about three hours, and went to a place in the station where refugees have to go. There were many English people there to give us breakfast and to help us. They were all very cheerful and smiling.

Some of the refugees looked ill and very unhappy and lost. There were children there without parents or relatives or friends. Some of the children were French and Belgian. There were several English doctors there and some spoke Dutch. They were helping to fix wounded people. Uncle Pieter has taken us to a hotel near the station. I am writing this in the hotel. Uncle Pieter says most of the Dutch and Belgium and French refugees are going to the country away from London so that if the bombs come again they will be safe. They will go to Ireland and Yorkshire and the Isle of Man and places like that where I have never been.

Uncle Pieter has gone away to send a cable to Uncle Klass in America and to see the American Counsul. Maybe we will go to America later, he says. If we do he is not going to go with us. He is going back to Holland. I suppose he has to get his car from the café-keeper and to tell father where we are. No one can send a cable to Holland now. You can send it but it doesn't do any good. It is fine to be in this country where it is so quiet and peaceful the way home was.

12: *The Diary of Dirk*

Later that day

Uncle Pieter came in with an English newspaper. I can read some of it easily. A funny thing happened. Queen Wilhelmina took a boat from Zeeland yesterday too. It is all written about in the English paper. The English King met her at Liverpool station and kissed her on both cheeks. Count Johan Paul van Limburg-Stirum, our minister to London, was there too. The Queen was probably very glad to see him but I didn't know she knew the English King well enough to let him kiss her on both cheeks. Crown Princess Juliana was there too, the paper says, and also Prince Bernhard and the Princess Beatrix who is two years old and Princess Irene who is just a baby.

There is a picture of them all in the paper and many soldiers standing around at attention. Some of them are Dutch soldiers. Princess Juliana is carrying Irene in her arms and Prince Bernhard and a nurse are carrying a box that the paper says is a gas-groof box for babies. It looks more like a puppy box than anything else. Little Beatrix must be in the box. Things must be very bad with our government if the Queen has come to England. Uncle Pieter says the Dutch government has moved from The Hague to London, the Cabinet and all. It must be hard to move the whole government. I imagine the Queen's boat was much larger than the one we came on. Yes, it was a battleship, the paper says. Keetje says she wishes we had come on the same boat with the Queen. So do I. Anyway we were in Zeeland at the same time.

Later that day

Uncle Pieter has just come back with terrible news. Holland has surrendered to the Germans. It is all in the newspapers. Uncle Pieter is almost crying. Ever since he came in he has been drinking and smoking and walking up and down. He says the fall of Holland threatens England and we must go to America if we can get a boat. Queen Wilhelmina, the paper says, is going to speak over the radio but we have no radio and cannot hear her. Uncle Pieter says maybe he won't be able to get back to Holland or find out any news of anything. I wonder where father is. I hope he is all right and safe and can go back to doctoring his animals. I just asked Uncle Pieter if we couldn't go back now that the war is over and he said never, never could we go back there while the Germans were there. He says it is worse than death for Hollanders to live as slaves. I hope the Germans don't make a slave out of father. I don't think they could. Father gets very angry and he would not stand for it.

Keetje is feeling very tired and ill. Uncle Pietre is having some food sent up to her, some warm milk and toast and eggs. I am having roast beef and pudding here with Keetje and Uncle Pietre is going to eat later. We haven't seen much of London yet and we have to stay inside tomorrow and rest. This is a very large room with high ceilings. Keetje and I stay in here and Uncle Pieter stays beyond the double doors. We have a private bath and it is very nice and quiet. The windows are all covered with thick cloth because it is after dark and no light must be shown because of the Germans. Keeje says she hopes

12: The Diary of Dirk

there won't be any noise tonight and that the Germans had better not come to London.

I wonder how the Baron and all our friends are. There was a dreadful bombing in Rotterdam today. The English newspaper says one third of the city was destroyed. The post office and out biggest building, a place called the beehive. It was mostly in the business section and along the wharves. I hope the bombs didn't come to our street. The Statendam, a big boat, caught fire and the Holland-American buildings were hit, Uncle Pieter says. Rotterdam is beautiful and I don't see why the Germans should want to tear it down and hurt the people who have never hurt them, Mother would have hated to hear about this. She loved Rotterdam almost as much as her home in Friesland. She met father the first time in Rotterdam before they married. Uncle Pieter says I must turn off the light now. He is going downstairs to the bar to get some more gin. He likes Schiedam. The Queen did not come over from Zeeland, Uncle Pieter says, but from Hook of Holland, so she was not near us after all!

Monday July 1, 1940

We have been in England many weeks. Now we are in Liverpool waiting for a boat to America. Uncle Pieter had heard from Uncle Klass in America and he wants Keeje and me to come. Uncle Klass had to cable the American Consul and his bankers in America had to do the same. Uncle Pieter had to get visas and things and all kinds of papers and pay a great deal of money, I think. A great fuss. We are having fun in England but we miss Holland. Keetje was ill for a week in the hotel in London. A doctor came to see her and said she was nervous. He gave her some medicine. He was very kind. He wouldn't let Uncle Pieter pay him anything. He said it was his pleasure and his gift to gallant Holland. Uncle Pieter says the English are just that way and good enough people when you know them.

Dear Uncle Pietre. He is so sad about Holland and so good to us. We have done so many things. In London he took us everywhere. The policemen-bobbies they are called!-are very funny and big and polite. We asked them many questions on walks when we got lost. We used to take taxis everywhere but now we use the little trams. All over London there are many things for war. Sand-bags everywhere. They were banked around the British Museum the day we went. The Museum had big pillars outside and many heavy doors before you get inside. Uncle Pieter was surprised to see so many people inside reading while there is a war on. There are many trenches everywhere and sand-bags at St. Paul's, a big church. In the gardens at Kensington there were many flowers but trenches too.

There are big black and white posters everywhere with ARP printed on them. This means Air Raid Precautions. People all carry gasmasks and we have them now. They were fitted on us by a nice woman in London. The gas masks have long snouts and look as funny as the Dutch ones. They have straps to hold them on. We must never carry them by the straps because they stretch and might let the gas in. That's what the woman said who gave them to us. Uncle Pieter put his on yesterday for the first time and looked at himself. He said he looked no better at all with it than without it. I laughed and he laughed too. I was glad to see him laugh for he has been so sad since he found out that one-fourth of our army was killed. When he reads the newspapers about the war he gets sadder and sadder. We haven't heard from father.

When Belgium fell Uncle Pieter was almost sick. I saw a funny dog today. It was an English sheep dog, Uncle Pieter said. Keetje thought it was a bear that had escaped from the zoo. Keeje asked if the animals had gas masks too and Uncle Pieter said no. It is a shame that they don't have. We had tea at the zoo with bread and butter and strawberry jam. I tasted Keetje's milk from the Baron's cows.

There are no street lights in England after dark. We are getting very tired of the dark but not as tired as we were. We have only been not as tired as we were. We have only been out once late at night. We were in a taxi with Uncle Pieter coming home from the Mickey Mouse cinema. There are no crossing lights except little shaded crosses no bigger than a button. It is very exciting going along in the dark. In the daylight we have gone into the country. The roads are all fixed to stop the Germans. There are many barricades and trenches and tank traps. We have seen many lorries in the streets filled with big searchlights and guns and soldiers.

My English is improving. I practice it on the chambermaid. So does Keetje. Keetje gets more practice than I do because everyone stops to talk with her. She is very cute-looking in her new sailor hat Uncle Pieter bought her. Uncle Pieter is trying to speak English with us too so that we can get used to it but he forgets half the time and talks Dutch. Liverpool is not so big as London. It has many boats, though, and we like to go down to the wharves because they remind us of dear Holland. We are staying at a big hotel named Adelphi. Everything in it is big. The bathtub is almost big enough to swim in and Keetje tried it and took a few strokes. The dining-room is big too.

Uncle Pieter has just come in with news. He says I must stop writing now. He has just had news from the ticket office that we have a passage and will leave sometime soon. He says he cannot go to see us off as it is against the rules because of the war. The ticket man is sending someone for us. I asked him the name of the boat and he said he didn't know that either because the ticket office couldn't let out any secrets out because of the Germans. I must stop and help Keetje and Uncle Pieter pack. I hate to leave England. I have had a good time here and I hope the Germans never do to England what they did to Holland. Good-by, England. We have to leave you just as we were beginning to love you. I suppose we will have to get used to having new homes since we can't go back to our own dear home in Holland.

Wednesday July 3, 1940

We are on the boat now. We sailed yesterday sometimes after dark. We had to wait many hours on the dock with the ticket man who told us animal stories. It was hard to leave Uncle Pieter. He kissed us many times and hugged us hard. He is going to let us know about father if he gets back to Holland. Uncle Klass will meet us in New York. We are on a big boat and there are many other children going to America. There are so many people going away because of the war that some of them have to sleep in bunks in the smoking rooms and halls. Everything is very strict on this English boat. Before we sailed a sailor told us what we could do and couldn't. We are not allowed on deck after the trumpet sounds in the evening. All the portholes are fastened tight and can't be opened. They are covered with thick cloths to blot out the light. The ship doesn't even have light on it to see by at night because of the submarines. The English sailor said no one could smoke on deck at night. A lighted cigarette can be seen two miles at sea, he says. If anyone disobeys he will be severely punished and put in a room and locked up for the rest of the trip.

There are double doors at the dining salon and we go in on the side so the lights don't show. There are many ships sailing beside us. We counted twenty. Six carry passengers and the rest are going to keep the submarines away. There are torpedo boats, warships, and one airplane carrier. They keep very near us all the time and we wave back and forth. The boats are all painted gray so they will be hard to see in the water. Everyone is afraid of the German submarines. The English Captain says for me not to worry because anyone who was born around as much water as we have in Holland just couldn't be drowned. He is a nice man and is always making jokes. There are two other Dutch children on the boat. They came from The Hague. Their father is working for the government. We speak Dutch together just to rest our tongues. We practice J's and th's on each other. Keetje has been seasick ever since we left but the Captain says she will be better when we get away from Ireland. He says he will be too because most of the submarines stay around here.

I have never been on such a big boat. I have been on many boats on canals but this one is like the Adelphi Hotel in Liverpool only it wobbles. A man was caught smoking a cigarette today and put him into a room and locked up just as the sailor said he would be. Many boys in Holland smoke at my age but I do not. There goes the bell for dinner and I am very hungry, and Keeje is pulling at my sleeve. She feels like eating tonight.

Saturday September 28, 1940

I have not written in my diary for so long. Not since I got to America. Uncle Klass and Aunt Helen met us. Aunt Helen is an American with long red fingernails and a very pretty face. Our boat came into New York at night on the tenth day after we left England. We came slowly because our boat had to take a longer way because of the war. We stayed all night in the harbor. We thought New York looked very exciting in the distance. There were so many lights and they were all on. All during the time we were in England there had never been any lights at night in the streets. It looked fine to see so many all going at once with so many colors. Uncle Krass took us off the boat the next morning without waiting.

12: The Diary of Dirk

Some of the children who were ill had to be taken off the boat somewhere else and some had gone to a place called Ellis Island.

When we got through the customs we drove to Uncle Klaas's apartment on Morningside Heights. The streets were very exciting. I remember particularly when we crossed one and Uncle Klass said this is Broadway. I came over here just to show you, he said. Aunt Helen said it is prettier at night. Uncle Klass has a beautiful apartment that is very near the river. Maybe he took it because he is Dutch and always wants to be near some water.

We have been in America several weeks now. Keetje and I go to a private school. We like it very much although it was strange at first. There were many new works and studies, but not so many languages to learn as in Holland. I am learning to play football and other sports. Keetje likes the movies and the drugstore sodas best. Keetje seems very happy. Sometimes I think she has forgotten about mother entirely. But I haven't. There is a girl in my glass who reminds me of M.v.R. and who is even prettier. She has brown eyes and hair and is named Betty Anne. Everyone is very kind to us and I have been made a monitor at school. School hours are shorter in America. My English has improved and I have learned many new words that I have never heard in England and some not in my dictionary.

Several letters have come from England from Uncle Pieter. He has not been able to get back to Holland. He is working for the English now and is a volunteering fire warden. Uncle Pieter says he misses us. He has had one letter from father and we have had one. Father is safe and back in Rotterdam. The letter we got from him had a Swiss stamp. It must now have been seen by the Germans, Uncle Klass says. Father tells about what Holland is like now. There is not much food and many things like coffee and cocoa cannot be bought. The Germans have done many things. They have changed the names of the Royal Museum and anything with the word royal in it to National. No taxis are running. None of the Dutch can listen on the radio to anything but Spanish, Italian and German programs without being fined 10,000 guildres and two years in prison. People have to stay home after 10 o'clock at night. The food is getting worse and worse. Father said not to worry, he would pull through. He wants to come to America. I wish he could and so does Keetje. We write to him often but we don't know whether he gets our letters. I will be so glad when the war is over.

Keetje and I are happy here and everything would be perfect if father and grandfather and grandmother were here and of course Uncle Pieter. I haven't had very good marks at school. The doctor says I am nervous and can't concentrate very well yet because of the bombing but that I will be all right later. The American doctor was just like the English one Uncle Pieter had for Keetje. He wouldn't charge any money for taking care of me. He said, this is on me, which is slang but very kind. I think he is a good doctor for I know I am nervous sometimes.

12: The Diary of Dirk

Sometimes when airplanes go over I want to run and hide. One night when it was raining I woke up and heard the rain on the glass and was frightened. I thought I was back in Holland and that what was striking the windows were pieces of bombs. That is why Uncle Klass doesn't like it when people ask me about the war. When he saw the theme I was trying to write in English class about the war in Holland he was angry. I heard him tell Aunt Helen that he thought it was dreadful and that he wanted Keetje and me to forget about the war. But I know I'll never forget about it anyway, or forget the Germans and how mother died. I won't forget America either. It is a good country that has made us feel welcome. Keetje is looking over my shoulder as I write this and says why don't you say its "swell," that's an American word.

I know one reason why I'll always love America. It's because of something that happened on the boat trip here. When we were one day away from New York all the battleships and boats that had brought us over so safely turned around and went back toward England. We were all alone and very frightened. I was frightened because I don't swim very well and Keetje can only do ten strokes and they don't get her very far. When the boats all turned back we could see how frightened everyone was. That's what made us frightened. We weren't frightened before. But then someone started yelling and pointing at the sky. There was a big zeppelin over us. It said United States Naval Patrol Number 14 in big letters. We all yelled and cheered. I won't ever forget that number 14, and the nice safe way it made us feel. The zeppelin followed us and watched over us all the rest of the way to America. And people have been watching over us ever since and there haven't been any bombings. Not one. And that is why Keetje and I are happy now.

CHAPTER 13: THE JOURNEY FOR LIFE

Ilse was born on December 25, 1925 in Stettin, Germany. Ilse was eight years old when Adolf Hitler became Fuhrer of Germany. Just two years later, at the tender age of 10, the anti-Semitism grew rampant and she endured taunting and harassment from classmates at school. By 1936, the Nuremberg laws were enacted and Ilse was banned from attending public school and was forced to enroll at the local Jewish school.

On November 9, 1938 the tragedy of Kristallnacht occurred and our family decided to leave Germany. I (Ilse) was placed on the Kindertransport list. While my parents planned to flee to Shanghai since a passport was not required. In the middle of winter, on January 1939 I bid farewell to my parents and left for Belgium. I was frightened and very sad to leave my family behind but my parents promised that soon we would be reunited again. I held on to that thought and left the only home that I ever knew.

Four months later, Germany and Belgium were at war. I was just beginning to adjust to life in Belgium but I, along with many other refugees, was sent to France to evade the war. The four day train ride was treacherous because German bombs exploded near by, but luckily the train safely arrived on May 18, 1940. Initially we lived primitively and the conditions were difficult on us. We were very scared and not used to living in such deplorable conditions. Then the Swiss Children's aid assisted us and in 1941 we were brought to a home called the Chateau de la Hille a much nicer place to live.

Subsequently, France declared war on Germany on September 3, 1939 when Germany invaded Poland. On August 26, 1942 the French police stormed into the Chateau de la Hille and forcibly took me along some of the other refugees. We were simply terrified! They sent us to an internment camp temporarily and we were to be deported to a concentration camp very soon. Frantically, the head of the Chateau, Rosali Naef contacted the Swiss Children's Aid and begged for our release. Thankfully after much prompting we were allowed to leave and we resumed residency at the Chateau. Mr. Naef along with the Swiss Children's Aid will always be remembered for their gracious deeds. I am now aware of what happened to people at concentration camps and I realize that I was quite fortunate to have survived.

Since the Germans now occupied France it became unsafe for us to remain there. Therefore, we were smuggled out of France and brought to Spain. It was difficult for all the children to leave at once so we fled slowly and often times in small groups so we were not conspicuous to others. Ultimately, we all crossed over the boarder into Switzerland and safely arrived in Spain. I (age 17) lived in several refugee camps but ultimately was placed with a protestant minister, Pastor Charles Brutsch. I was then hired to be their au pair but graciously Mr. Brutsch treated me with love and compassion and I became a part of their family.

13: The Journey for Life

I longed for the day when I would be reunited with my parents. So much time had elapsed but they remained a constant thought in my mind every single day. Sadly, the news arrived that my father died in Shanghai in 1940 and towards the end of the war mother died from typhus. The news of their death devastated me and I felt very alone.

At age 14, she left on the Kindertransport. After evading the Nazis for three solid years, she finally settled in Spain. She continued to live with the Minister and their family for the next several years and eventually earned a pediatric nursing degree. Still, she always felt very hurt because she never got to see her parents again. God bless them.

Postcard sent to Annelise Wasserman by her father while she was on the Kindertransport. Sadly, her father died shortly after mailing this letter. (Courtesy USHMM)

CHAPTER 14: THE WASSERMAN FAMILY

Eugen and Nanetter (Joelsohn) Wasserman were blessed with two wonderful children: Annelise, born in 1921, and Ruth, born on May 20, 1926. They owned a prosperous leather manufacturing company and lived a traditional Jewish life in

Nuremberg, Germany. Adolf Hitler ordered a boycott against Jewish shops in 1933 and as a result their business lost large accounts and ultimately closed.

As Adolf Hitler was waving a war of persecution upon Germany, my father Eugene Wassermann was fighting his own battle; his health was deteriorating considerably as he was diagnosed with tuberculosis. Simultaneously, the Nazis organized a statewide boycott of all Jewish shops, they blocked patrons from the entrance way of stores and frightened citizens from conducting business with the Jewish community. Our leather business suffered as a result of the imposed sanctions and our once prosperous business was lagging in sales.

To supplement our debilitating income we moved out of our comfortable house and leased it out. We resided in a smaller more affordable apartment while hoping that the boycott would cease to interrupt our business and prosperity would bless us again. But the persecution continued to sweep across Germany and we were forced to liquidate our business.

In April of 1937, two years after closing our business, we moved to Berlin with the hope that my father would become a cosmetic manufacturer and rekindle his business spirit in a land where opportunity would not hinder him based on his religious affiliation. But less than two years later, Berlin endured the dreadful night of Kristallnacht and dad was arrested and sent to Alexanderplatz where my mom followed his tracks and delivered his medication personally to him despite the dangerous trek.

14: The Wasserman Family

Upon arrival at home, mom was devastated to find her youngest daughter Ruth bottled over in severe pain. She urgently tried to locate a doctor who would treat her, but many of the physicians had been arrested and taken to concentration camps as so many Jewish men were on Kristallnacht. Eventually they located a physician who diagnosed her as having appendicitis. Her condition was acute and required her to be operated on immediately. Ruth endured a successful operation the following day at the local Catholic hospital.

Concurrently, dad's health concerns were so substantial that the Nazis sent him home because he was physically incapable of enduring the harsh physical labor that the concentration camp demanded. After tolerating the soaring persecution from Germany to Berlin we grew quite determined to get out of the path of the Nazis.

After contacting an Uncle in London, my parents arranged to have their girls participate in the Kindertransport. On April 8, 1939 Ruth and I traveled to England and was taken to the Bloomsbury House located in London. I who was actually teetering on being 18 years old was appointed to do domestic work while my younger sister Ruth went to a foster home. The home proved unsuccessful for Ruth therefore she was sent to the youth hostel in London, Hackney.

With the war threatening London the children in the hostel were evacuated to Cockley Clef in Norfolk which is a rural area. Ruth remained in Norfolk until the fall of 1941 but eventually was sent to Bnai Brith a hostel located in London where she would begin working, as she was now approaching fifteen.

Almost two years since my parents sent us away they finally secured their own way out of Berlin. They boarded the trans-Siberian railway to Vladivostok which is situated at the chief Russian seaport. They proceeded on to Kobe, Japan where they stayed for a short time until they found availability on the Japanese freighter which sailed from Tokohama to South America. After forty nine days at sea they finally arrived in Panama on September 14, 1940.

Three months after arriving on the shores of Panama and finally securing safety, their father died on December 4, 1940. Two months later, Nanette continued her journey alone and immigrated to the United States. As a widow in a foreign land, she worked as a domestic to sustain herself. After the war ended, Nanette's children, now all grown up, traveled to the United States, and reunited with their mother. They rekindled their relationship with their mother and mourned the death of their father.

Han Schneider just before boarding a plane. His father's arm is resting on his back. (Courtesy Han Schneider)

CHAPTER 15: THIRTY TURBULENT MONTHS

Hans Schneider was born into an upper middle-class family in Vienna, Austria. His parents, Hugo and Isabella, gladly welcomed their healthy newborn son in 1927. Hans, an only child, was an inquisitive, bright-eyed boy, who excelled in mathematics and thrived academically. His mother and father were both prosperous dentists in Vienna. When the Germans occupied Austria, Hugo's thriving private dental practice was seized by the Nazis. It was evident that the Nazis were attempting to invade all of Europe. Almost immediately thereafter, their comfortable lifestyle became filled with curfews, restrictions, persecution, and continuous fear. Out of sheer desperation, Mr. Schneider made the bold and daring decision to flee to Czechoslovakia despite not having the proper paperwork, and that courageous move saved their lives. The family then fled to

Poland. When Poland became unsafe, Hans left to go to the Netherlands, where he was to be enrolled in a Quaker School, but his 10-day airline delay almost became his demise. Hans eventually reunited with his parents in Scotland. However, in the interim, they traveled hundreds of miles and passed through numerous countries, all in an effort to elude the invading Nazis, and somehow they managed to survive.

The difficult and painful memories for Hans as a youngster have been embedded in his subconscious for decades. He used to remark, "I was born in Edinburgh at the age of 12," a joke with serious content, "Until I reached my late sixties, I claimed that I had no recollection whatsoever of the first eleven years of my life- and believed it. My prenatal existence was hard to admit and remains shadowy in spite of a conscious effort to recapture it".

When the German army marched into Austria in March 1938, my father expected a return to some kind of ghetto existence. Both my parents were dentists in Vienna: my mother, Bella (Isabella), worked for the municipal dental service inspecting school children, and my father, Hugo, had a successful private practice. My father believed that he would lose all his non-Jewish patients; on the other hand many Viennese Jews went to non-Jewish dentists, and some would now come to him: not good, but tolerable. Within three months he realized that he had been quite wrong. The immediate cause was the appearance of a young man at his door in SA uniform who announced that he was also a dentist and one of my parents' two consulting rooms now belonged to him.

15: Thirty Turbulent Months

I was 11 years old in 1938. At this remove, I have a sense that I was quite aware of restrictions and possible dangers in the three months that I lived under Nazi rule, but nevertheless my daily activities continued much as before. On one occasion, I remember being called out into the courtyard of my school with all other boys of Jewish descent and being told by the headmaster that it was impossible for true Germans to associate with us, and he probably added some less than complimentary words about the group in front of him. My parents reacted by remarking: First this man was red (which meant a supporter of the moderate social democrats that ran the city until 1934), then black (a supporter of the Catholic oriented government that took over Austria in 1934), and now he is brown (a Nazi). Wise words, they stopped me from taking seriously anything he may have said.

My father was a very careful and cautious man, yet he took an extraordinarily bold action which was crucial to our survival. In June 1938 we took a train to Czechoslovakia. As the Nazis' aim was to drive out Jews, leaving Austria was possible and legal, but the difficulty of getting permission to enter another country was huge. In our case, a Czech border guard had been bribed and we entered the country illegally. Thus ended what had been a secure middle class existence up to the annexation of Austria by Germany, and we became refugees without resources, status or prospects; three lives in limbo. My parents and I went to live with one of my father's brothers in Karvina, the town where my father was born. This town was very close to the Polish border and it was ceded to Poland by the Munich agreement in late 1938, and thus we found ourselves illegally in Poland.

In the fall of 1938, my parents managed to get a place for me in a Quaker school in the Netherlands which had been established for German and Austrian refugee children. I had to travel to Warsaw to obtain a visa from the Dutch consul there and then, to get to Holland without entering Germany, I would need to take a plane to Prague and then a plane direct to Amsterdam. But the first plane could not leave because of bad weather, there was a wait of 10 days for the next available seat on the plane from Prague and no hotel would take a person without papers. My father, who was accompanying me, had to find a way for me to stay in Warsaw. He asked the first reliable looking man he saw in the street for help, who sent us to a member of the German embassy in whose apartment I then stayed. Equally amazing, the man who sent us there turned out to be a Polish policeman in the very department charged with deporting illegal aliens. I presume there was an anti-Nazi underground in both organizations. This is one of the few stories my father would tell about our experiences; surely the family I stayed with was German and I was told to say that I was a relative from Vienna if anyone asked. In 2005 I received several letters which my mother. She was pleading for me to be granted an entry permit to the Netherlands where I would then join the Quaker School.

Here is a letter written on November 24, 1938 by my mother to the Quaker School.

15: Thirty Turbulent Months

Dear Mrs. Coster
Please don't be angry that I ask you to speed up the matter. Our situation here is so uncertain that I hardly know whether an acceptance that occurs only after a few weeks would still find us here. We are here completely dependent on our relatives who themselves do not know how their situation will develop in the next few weeks. This is how we would be so glad to know that our child has reached safety.

Should this matter be delayed for some time despite your kind efforts then it would help us greatly if you knew of a Dutch family in Poland (in Warsaw or elsewhere) who would be ready to keep Hansl until his departure.

While living with my uncle in Karvina, my parents were denounced to the authorities, but the local police, instead of deporting them back to Germany according to regulations, allowed them 24 hours to flee to the interior of Poland. There they again lived illegally with distant relatives and waited for British or American visas, whichever would come first. In April 1939, my father was one of about 40 German or Austrian dentists permitted to enter Britain, which my parents reached by boat from Poland. They lived in London for some months, but there was pressure from the refugee organizations for the refugees to disperse to other parts of the country. My parents chose to move to Edinburgh where I rejoined them in August 1939, just before the outbreak of war. I do not know if I realized during our separation that I might never see them again. I imagine my parents must have had such thoughts, but I do not know for sure, for the events I am writing about here, or even our previous lives in Vienna, were never discussed later.

Here is a letter written by my mother on October 29, 1938

We received an order to leave this country within 48 hours. This order was then changed; we may stay until November 9th. It would be our greatest good fortune if the matter of Hansl were settled by then.

We are infinitely greatful to you for your efforts and I wish I could prove this to you some day.

In retrospect, I see the decision to leave Austria as a huge gamble. Had my parents not been in a town annexed by Poland before the German invasion of Czechoslovakia in March 1939, had the Nazis invaded Poland six months earlier, or had Polish policemen not acted contrary to their duty on two occasions, their fates and mine would have ended very differently. Our survival was a mixture of skillful and decisive action, and extraordinary good luck. My father urged his brother to give up his clothing store and to leave for the west. I do not think he tried to do so, but, even if he did, it is highly unlikely that any country would have admitted my uncle, his wife and young son in time. They were killed in the holocaust, a fate that seems particularly poignant as my father's eldest brother fell fighting for Austro-Hungary in World War I.

There was a second disruption of my parents' lives. In May 1940 Germany invaded the Low Countries and France, and a rumor swept Britain that their rapid progress was due to the help of German spies disguised as refugees. My father, who had just managed to complete his examinations for dental surgery which he required to exercise his profession again, was interned like all other German or Austrian refugee men living in Edinburgh, a town considered sensitive in view of its location on the East coast. All had previously been classified by a British tribunal as "friendly enemy aliens". My mother was not interned but had to leave Edinburgh and went to live with three or four other refugee women in one room in Glasgow, while I (being under 16) could stay in Edinburgh and attend one of the best schools there, living with a single Scottish lady of independent means (who later took in several Austrian and Hungarian refugee boys who had reached Scotland without their parents). Sometimes I think this may have been the worst part of my parents' lives as they were forcibly separated. While my father was interned on the Isle of Man, some refugees were transported to Canada, and one such ship was sunk by a German U-Boat. It was several weeks before my mother heard that my father was safe. I do not think that such thoughts occurred to me at the time, then aged 13. I was focused on doing well at my academically oriented school and I am still grateful for the education I received.

My father was released from internment in August 1940 largely through the efforts of the Church and some members of Parliament. He was among the first; dentists were needed since many had been conscripted to serve in the armed forces. He established a practice in Edinburgh and thus ended a period when we had been supported by charity, living in two rooms in some landlady's flat. My mother did not attempt to resume her professional life; I do not know why. During the next five years we shared the experience of the British people at war, a remarkable people whom the world owes gratitude for their decision in September 1939 to fight Hitler. For a teenager, this was an exciting time; though I was an avid reader of newspapers, I did not realize the full horror of it until the war was over.

I have already mentioned that the past was never discussed in my family in subsequent years. As a postscript I'd like to give an explanation. In my opinion, the reason is not at all that thinking about the past was unbearably painful, for I was aware that up to the German annexation of Austria we had led a privileged life compared with the great majority of mankind, whatever the difficulties that I may have been unaware of as a child. Rather, there was a tremendous need for assimilation and adaptation to our new lives in Scotland, particularly for me as a teenager. Attachment to a dead past is a burden when coping with the difficulty of rebuilding your life in a new country; for many years our eyes were firmly fixed on the present and future.

While in Scotland Hans Schneider married another Kindertranportee Miriam Wieck in 1948. Miriam is a violinist, and prolific musician. Hans received his Ph. D. in mathematics in 1952 and currently lives in Wisconsin where he is a Professor at the University of Wisconsin-Madison. His father Hugo reestablished himself as a dentist in Edinburgh, Scotland. In 1968 after a 46 year marriage they both perished in Scotland.

✫ ✫ ✫

CHAPTER 16: SCHINDLER OF BRITAIN

When Adolf Hitler occupied Czechoslovakia, he and his soldiers systematically deprived, humiliated, and economically disempowered Jews before sending them to the confines of concentration camps. Eva and her sister Vera were teenagers in 1938, on the brink of deportation when one young man miraculously changed the course of their lives.

The English stockbroker Nicholas Winton was on a holiday leave and about to vacation in Switzerland. Instead, he canceled his trip and went to Prague in the winter of 1938 with his friend Martin Blake and embarked on one of the most urgent rescues of his time. Upon touring Prague, he was horrified at the terrible conditions at the refugee camps and clearly foresaw the eminent danger that loomed for the children and therefore felt compelled to do something about it. He set up an office in a hotel in Wenceslas Square in Prague and accepted each youngster one by one over a two week period in an effort to save their lives. He guaranteed visas and adoption papers, raised the required 50-pound fee (U.S. dollars $1,500), and managed to override bureaucratic formalities. Over a nine-month period, Winton saved the lives of 669 children who fled their homeland without their parents and were welcomed by the kindness and generosity of the people of Great Britain.

Although some of the children today recall the rescue process, they had no idea who the man was behind the mission. The miraculous rescue went unrecognized for five decades. In

1988, Nicholas's wife, Grete, noticed a leather briefcase in their attic. Upon inspection, she saw lists of names and letters from parents, and she was puzzled by her discovery. In the end, Mr. Winton, now in his late 80s, somewhat bashfully revealed the rescue that he had organized so many years ago.

Nicholas Winton is regarded as the "Schindler of Britain," a reference to Oskar Schindler, who managed to save 1,000 Jews from Germany. They both possessed fortitude and dedication and risked their own lives for the sake of humanity. Eve and Vera are forever grateful to Winton's generosity and goodwill, and they personally reiterated this to him when they met some years ago. This is the account of one of "Winton's children." This is Eva's story.

My parents will send their love by the moon and the stars were my mother's (Irma Diamantova) last words to me at the station in Prague on the 29th of June 1939. And that I should write about my experiences, my thoughts and feelings in a diary given to me by him, was the wish of my Father, Karel Diamant.

A year earlier no one in our happy family expected that my country, called Czechoslovakia, would be invaded by the German army. I was called Eva and was born on the 1st of January 1924. We lived in a small town called Celakovice, swam in the river Elb in the summer, skated on the same river in the winter, went skiing in the mountains (Krkonose), were Jewish, but not very religious, though a rabbi came from Prague once a fortnight to teach us about Judaism.

My sister Vera and I went to the only local primary school which was mainly Roman Catholic. I remember helping my friends collect "sins" before their confession and liking their priest because he always had sweets in his pocket. What religion one belonged to did not seem important in our community. "To love you and your sister and Mother, to do good in this world, is my religion, said my Father when I asked him what he believed.

He and Mother were extremely generous to everyone and were held in high esteem by the people in our township. Both worked very hard in our business, manufacturing wine and liquors, to give us a good life. Father and Mother participated in the life around us. When the footballers won their game Father sent them a crate of beer to celebrate, when they lost the same gift was sent – for them to drown their sorrow.

I dearly loved both my parents but Father was my idol. I remember our walks by the river, no topic was forbidden. He and I were followed by my mother and sister, who joked and laughed, Vera, 4 years my junior, was full of fun and mischief, a delightful blue eyed girl.

My eyes were black and I was thought to be very serious!!

Life was good, and I was aware of it, aware how fortunate I was to have my family and my many friends.

This life came drastically to an end on the 15th of March 1939 when my country was invaded and fear became visible all around us. Mother was hurriedly storing food etc because shops were soon depleted by the German army – and who knew what the future held??

There were soldiers everywhere, in our school, even our "third" room was occupied by them.

The 10,000 Children That Hitler Missed

That Jews were persecuted in Germany and Austria for no other reason except that they were Jews this was going to happen in my country. Racism showed its ugly head.

When my parents found out about Nicholas Winton, a young Englishman who gave up his holidays in order to rescue as many, mainly Jewish, children as possible by organizing transport, visas, permits, families etc to get us to England, they gave him our names etc. Vera and I were "fortunate "to be chosen for the transport to England.

I was aware at the age of 15, what this decision must have cost my parents who adored us. We were leaving them, our grandparents, uncles and aunts, leaving our cousins and many friends. At midnight at the station in Prague, 200 children were boarding a train to a country they knew not, whose language they could not speak, going to people they knew not, nor did they know how long for. In spite of this uncertainty, in spite of their pain, our parents gave us life the second time. And those in England who offered us a home knew us not, nor did they know how long we shall be staying, they only saw our photographs, but did not know whether we would be good or naughty etc.

From the train ride I remember mainly having cocoa in Holland I was also hiding a little elephant, little cross and a Jewish medallion which, together, were hanging on a little chain round my neck, hiding them from the German guards who came to inspect us before allowing us to leave the German border. From Holland we sailed to Harwich. But vividly I remember waking up in the morning and seeing the sunrise on the water, my first glimpse of the sea, it was love at first sight which remained with me to this day.

Only vaguely can I bring to mind the trip to London where I had to part with my sister who eventually finished with a loving family in Liverpool while I was met by a teacher from a boarding school in Branksome, Dorset. I was the only foreigner, no one else was Jewish. This was an Anglican school and the owners gave me free board and education. The headmistress, Miss Dunn, was responsible for my daily needs. I went to the Anglican Church with the rest of the girls, believing there was only One God, and how we prayed was secondary to how we lived. Anyhow, I could not understand what was said - so I spent the hour thinking of home.

I worked hard, as instructed by my father, learned English quickly, passed any exams with flying colors and was extremely lonely inspite of being surrounded by kindness.

I spoke to no one of my fears for my parents once the war broke out and letters from home ceased.

I tried to be of help to my sister with whom, thanks to our guardians we met during our holidays. She was fortunate to get a place in the one and only Czech school in England and so was among her own.

I wrote diligently in my diary. I also left a diary at home, one that no one read till after our departure, when my father asked for permission to read it – I willingly gave this. I had written there among other joys and sorrows and fears, of my great love for my parents, of my awareness of this their great sacrifice when they decided to send us to England , how much I was grateful to them for all that they have given us.

My aunt, who survived the war, told me what a great comfort this was to them.

After nearly 3 years at school I went to nursing school in Poole, survived all the bombing we had, was determined not to fall in love inspite of boyfriends for I wanted to be free to return home after the war. This I did, both Vera and I went back – knowing that both our parents as well as most of our relatives perished in the Holocaust.

Eventually both Vera and I returned to England. With my heart belonging to two countries, life seemed confusing. Till I met and married a doctor, Michael Hayman and in 1957 with our two children, Simon and Joanna, we immigrated to New Zealand.

After my children left the university I commenced my studies and received my MA.

When wanting to throw away my diaries, written for my parents during the war, the parents who were never to read them, my daughter Joanna asked me to translate them instead. This I did – into a very condensed edition – of BY THE MOON AND THE STARS.

This helped to ease some of the pain, which was forever mine, though I had my own much loved family. This family has grown by Simon's partner Tirsa in Denmark, and Joanna's husband Peter and their two children, Jeff and Nadia, joys of my life. I am forever grateful that they live in Auckland.

I also had the privilege on a number of occasions, when visiting my sister, to meet Nicholas Winton, and

16: Schindler of Britain

thank him for my life. Because one man struggled to save 664 children, because kind people cared and because our parents loved us with so unselfish a love which gave them the courage to send us away, here am I, at the age of 83 - grateful for the lives of those who are mine. Surely here is a lesson to learn – at any age.

In 2007 there are 5,000 descendents from the 669 rescued children. Eva published her story in her book titled, By The Moon And The Stars and she continues to live in New Zealand and counts her blessings everyday. Her sister Vera started a family and remained in England. Their mother died in Bergen-Belsen after liberation and their father died from a hunger march. In 2002 Nicholas Winton received a knighthood by Queen Elizabeth II. His wife, Grete who originally found the briefcase and uncovered this story recently passed away.

CHAPTER 17: SONJA'S CHERISHED DIARY

Sonja Herzberg was a brown-haired girl with a radiant smile, mature, resilient and strong willed. She is gregarious and had many girlfriends while growing up in Cologne, Germany. After the violence of Kristallnacht on November 9/10th 1938, Sonja realized that the Nazis were capable of massive destruction, and she feared for the safety of her family. She fled Germany in the fall of 1939 on the Kindertansport. Once in England, she often daydreamed, staring into oblivion while secretly wishing that she was back in her parent's arms feeling their warm embrace around her. At times, the absence of her family brought many sleepless nights to the young teen, but she possessed a resilience that helped her to overcome her hardship. The kindness of the English people always brought comfort to her mind and eased the pain during her transition. Sonja began her little blue diary/ autograph book as a student in Germany. It became a symbol of the treacherous life that many of her friends endured. When she realized the fate that was eminent to the ones who stayed behind, it placed an unheralded hardship on her mind. She carried the diary until her dying day. This is Sonja's story.

I was born on October 31, 1924 to Regina and Leopold Herzberg and named Sonja Feigel Herzberg. We were a middle-class orthodox Jewish family and I was an only child. At the age of thirteen, in the fall of 1937, I received a gift from my parents that I would possess until my dying day—a little blue adorned with a big red bow. That diary became a staple of my adolescent years while living in Germany and then during my exile in England.

I was a popular girl in grade school, but due to the Nuremburg laws I was forced out of the public school system and sent to the Lutzowstrasse Jewish School in Cologne, Germany. I was sad to leave all my friends behind, and eventually my gentile friends stopped speaking to me entirely. One day, I decided to bring my diary to school and have my dear friends sign it, and I continued that traditions for several years. They incorporated wonderful short poems and I have looked back on their words my entire life.

When the SS would march outside our home, my mother always ushered me away from the window, but I peered though the curtains and caught a glimpse of the men who would someday destroy our lives. They seemed to hate Jews for no reason at all. We were no different than them, but somehow they felt superior. They shuffled around Germany with their crisp uniforms and swastika armbands and treated Jews like inferior beings, including little children. It was apparent that they were brainwashed to think that we were different, and of course they were wrong. I once saw an SS soldier on the street holding a measuring device to determine the size of one man's skull. I later learned that the shape of a head made a significant difference in determining who was inferior or superior according to the Aryan philosophy.

I remember the SS holding signs up in front of the Jewish owned businesses that read, "Don't buy from Jews." Whenever someone walked in front of the store-

17: Sonja's Cherished Diary

front, they gave them a look, as if to say, "You better not enter this store, or else!" Many of my friends eventually lost their once-successful shops either because the Nazis confiscated them or they simply lost their clients.

When I was 15, my mother sat me down and explained to me that I was going to England to escape the brutality that had fallen upon Germany. I will never forget the look in her eyes, the fear, the uncertainty, and the sadness. She promised that we would be reunited soon, but I doubted her words. She called me her little princess and gave me a look of love that still permeates through my soul and makes me feel like her one and only baby. Still, I felt brokenhearted at the thought of leaving my home, family, and all that I knew. I also felt that it was unfair to be forced out of my country just because I was Jewish.

I arrived in Britain on August 23, 1939. I felt like a fish out of water. The surrounds looked completely different, the customs and food were foreign, and deep down I just wanted to run away. The initial phase of adjustment was hard on me because I desperately missed home. I soon realized that I had to accept the predicament I was in, but it baffled me that not even my own parents could save me. I later learned that they actually were saving me by sending me away. I resided in Gwrych Castle in Northeast Wales for several years then lived in the Kinneresley house. The castle had no running water or electricity, and the rudimentary living conditions were difficult on us all. I met many new friends while living in the castle, and they declared their thoughts in my diary up until the dispersal in 1941.

On September 3, 1939 at precisely 11:15 a.m., Neville Chamberlain (Prime Minister of Great Britain) declared war on Germany, and our lives were never the same again. We practiced for blackout conditions several months before the war broke out so that enemy planes were not able to easily identify targets. We would drape sheets or blankets over the windows, and we had to cover every single crevice so not a smidgen of light could seep through. We were instructed on how to place the gas mask over our face in case the Germans dispersed chemical warfare against us. The streets were pitch black, and the lights in our home were dim or we used candles. Air raid wardens would patrol the streets to notify the civilians if they were not properly following the blackout procedures.

A loud siren would erupt to warn the civilians that potential bombs were near. We ran to our bomb shelter for safety. As I sat there in the shelter, I looked up, pictured the heavens in my mind, and prayed that my family would somehow survive this terrible war. I called it the war against the Jews because it seemed that for some strange reason we were targeted by the Nazis. The shelter looked like an underground igloo but was disguised with greenery. I know it was good for us to be shielded within the shelter, but it was scary and I could feel my heart beating furiously in my blouse each and every time we entered.

I remember turning seventeen. I had a crush on one of the boys who lived down the street. He was not a

17: Sonja's Cherished Diary

refuges but from a prominent English family. One day, when my eyes caught his, he said hello and smiled. He grinned and had adorable deep dimples, and I simply melted. I noticed him several months prior, but I did not dare say a word to him, or anyone else for that matter, about my affection. One day, he invited me into his posh home. It was a magnificent castle filled with lavish antiques. Opulent chandeliers hung in the foyer and I found myself staring into the crystals as they cast off a rainbow of colors against the sunlight. His name was Peter, and we both enjoyed art and the same music. We shared countless stories together about life and religion. One day, when I told him about my family back in Germany, he insisted that he and I would go back there when the war was over and he would rescue them. When he told me this, I felt like he was my shining armor, and our eyes meet. His glistened against the sun, and I batted my long eyelashes back. Passion filled the room and a sign of cupid was emerging. He was very sweet.

On occasion, I would eat dinner at Peter's house. One particular day, I fixed my hair extra special and wore a nice dress, which hung to my knees. Peter complimented me on my attire and we laughed and talked for many hours. The dining room was adorned with a gold gilded mirror with lion heads protruding from the frame. The room was empty, as everyone had finished the scrumptious dinner. I glanced in the mirror and saw my reflection, and Peter walked in. He looked into the mirror and stared at me. It was a look of desire. I was beaming, and my body felt filled with passion. I could feel his emotions, and I simply wanted to turn to him and share my affection. But I grew scared and ushered myself out of the room immediately. My feelings frightened me and I ran home.

The next morning, I received a letter in the mail. I opened it quickly because I thought that it was from my parents. Instead, it was a letter from the Red Cross. The letter was short and read as follows. "Leopold and Regina Herzberg's whereabouts are unknown." I knew that meant they were killed in the Holocaust. Those letters were given to a few of my friends about their loved ones. I feel to my knees screamed and cried for hours. Then lay on the living room floor all night trying to grasp the reality. I stayed in the house for weeks, my eyes were swollen, and I had trouble sleeping and eating. The deep sadness immobilized me: it was like the wind was taken out of my sails and my heart was forever broken. I was sad, hurt, and angry all at the same time. The news was shocking, but I heard rumors of the horrendous concentration camps and was plagued with the thought that my parents endured the sadistic torture the Nazis imposed on so many. Peter tried to be a comfort but I simply did not want to see him, or anyone for that matter. I changed after I found out about my parents' deaths. I was quiet, reserved, and untrusting.

I anticipated the reunion in my mind a million times. My dad with outstretched arms with my mother's creamy complexion drenched with tears and joy. The hugs and kisses would overwhelm me with pleasure, and we would resume our lives and live happily ever after. But the reality was far from the truth. After living in Britain for 10 years, I decided to move away and start a

17: Sonja's Cherished Diary

new life. Peter and I remained good friends, and I know he was crushed when I told him about moving away, but I was ready to put my painful past behind me.

On January 18, 1949, at the age of 25, I immigrated to Israel, the Promised Land, and left the country that had saved me from the horrors of war. I packed my little blue diary once again; it was filled to capacity with the memories of my distant past and possessed the aura of my dear parents.

Sonja lived the rest of her life in Israel and died in her early eighties, her testimony was based on the recollections of a childhood friend. She kept in contact with Peter and they remained cherished friends. Peter always imagined them getting married. He never quite got over her leaving. Her diary was found in Israel in 2006, almost 70 years after Sonja had received it as a gift from her mother. After extensive research, the diary revealed the catastrophic reality that most of the children who signed it were victims of the Nazis. Their words convey the emotional strife that plagued them. The children were between the ages of 12-16, and most died before they reached their eighteenth birthday. Their thoughts reveal their innermost fears and their desire to weather any storm while their lives were crumbling apart around them. For most of the teenagers, their poems are their last surviving words.

✫ ✫ ✫

The 10,000 Children That Hitler Missed

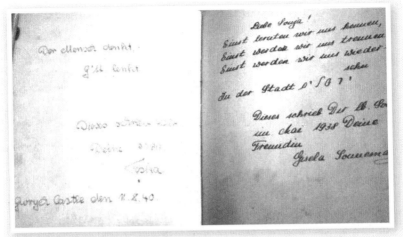

Sonja Herzberg began her diary in 1939 at the age of fifteen. Fifty-seven friends declared their poems from 1937–1941. Most were victims of the Holocaust. (Courtesy- private collection of Lori Greschler)

Sonja's Little Blue Diary-
The entries from Sonja's diary are particularly moving. As current observers, we get a glimpse into the lives of children who lived over three scores ago and suffered unimaginable hardship. Their eyewitness accounts reveal the earlier days in Hitler's reign and provide a glimpse into the unconscionable tragedies that unfolded. The voices of the 1.5 million children who were ruthlessly murdered in the Holocaust were stifled, but these poems keep their memories alive as we sift through their sparse words and ponder.

Entries from Cologne, Germany and the children who were victims of The Holocaust:
-1937-

17: Sonja's Cherished Diary

By the time the children wrote their diary message in 1937, the Nuremberg laws had been institutionalized for a few years already, and non-Aryans were disenfranchised and separated from German society in a variety of ways. Marriage and/or sexual relations between Jews and Aryans were strictly forbidden and Jews were no longer considered citizens of Germany. All Jewish-owned property was registered with the government and Jewish workers or managers were let go; thus many businesses were confiscated by the Nazis. Jewish doctors were only permitted to administer treatment to other Jews while lawyers were disbarred. As a whole, the Jewish community was gradually being alienated from society and prevented from earning a livelihood. Jewish households could not employ German domestic workers or display the Reich flag. They were not permitted in public pools, playgrounds, recreational facilities, or public schools. Jews found it difficult to purchase food or buy medicine for their sick children, as many shop owners had signs that read, "Jews Not Admitted." The laws were stringently enforced and, if not adhered to, people were arrested and ultimately sent to a concentration camp. By 1937, the Buchenwald concentration camp was opened, and initially political prisoners occupied the barracks. Soon it would be filled with Jews and other groups targeted by the Nazis. The Jews became easy targets for the Nazis since they were required to carry cards that revealed their religious affiliation. Everyone in Germany was ordered to carry an identification card; however, if one was deemed Jewish, a red "J" was added to their card and their middle name was changed to "Israel" for a man or "Sara" for a woman if their names were not easily recognizable as "Jewish names."

Diary entries 1937-

November 4, 1937   Carla Horn

Learn to endure reproaches, let people tell you the truth, never complain about it, it hurts but it does you good.

November 4, 1937   Trudy Benjamin

Near a quiet pond, a flower grows, small and brave and at the sound of the wave it whispers: "Forget me not"!

November 8, 1937   Miriam Bombas

If some day in many years you will be reading this book again, remember how happy we were when we were children happily rushing to class.

November 9, 1937   Toni Meyer

You must learn how to be docile, and respect your mother's world. Learn to speak, learn to be silent but do it only when you ought. Be fair to the young and modest to the old. Learn to avoid all evil. I know that's more than gold.

November 10, 1937   Renate Balder

My humble poem is very short. I'm just writing: forget me not! Renate was born in 1926 and perished in the Holocaust.

17: Sonja's Cherished Diary

November 11, 1937   Manfred

Always be purposeful and strive for the good then you will always be fine.

No date   Margot Drucken

The one who plays with life can never get it right. If you don't rule over yourself you'll always be a knight.

October 4, 1937   Karla Levy

Sixty minutes has an hour, more than thousand has a day. Oh my son, let me remind you, that there is no time to waste!

-1938 -
Sonya's diary was graced with wishes from twenty-one friends in 1938 while the violence of Kristallnacht was looming near by and anti-Semitism was soaring. Adolf Hitler and his henchmen had infiltrated the minds of many since his inception five years prior. The year brought the horrible reality that violence and persecution would haunt anyone who was not 100% Arian. The Germans annexed Austria and tormented the 190,000 Jews who lived there. Jewish-owned property was confiscated, bank accounts were taken over by the Nazis, and Aryans occupied the vacated homes. The Austrians were caught in the tightly woven web of maltreatment, and forced emigration, which caused an international refugee crisis. The Evian Conference was held to address the influx of people in exile, but 39 nations and 34 relief agencies all decided to close their

doors. *The Dominican Republic offered to accept some Jews under the Sosua Project and approximately 500 Jews sought exile there. Hitler soon realized that immigrating the Jews to other countries was not a reality; therefore, he devised other schemes to dispose of them-the final solution. In addition to Austria, the Nazis seized parts of Czechoslovakia and were planning a far-reaching attempt to conquer the world. In the interim, a sea of concentration camps opened throughout Germany and Jews were incarcerated daily.*

By November 10, 1938, twenty-four hours of violence plagued over fifty cities in Germany and Austria as the Nazis maliciously torched the cities and arrested 30,000 men. Josef Goebbels, a propaganda wizard under Adolf Hitler, masterminded Kristallnacht. The bloodshed resulted in numerous deaths of innocent people and catastrophic violence that plagued cities for decades. Most of the temples that were desecrated that night are still not rebuilt today. The emotional brutality still lives with the survivors and tormented the young children who wrote their sweet poems in Sonya's diary.

17: Sonja's Cherished Diary

Diary Entries 1938-

May 19, 1938   Helga Salm

Forget the hours of trouble, but never forget what they have taught you!

May 19, 1938   Gisela Block

Do your things, god will do his.

June 1938   Klara Hebor

Jewish you were born, Jewish you have to be, Once the Jews got lost and then they became Free!

July 12, 1938   Rufi Vogelhut

I'm writing in your album so that you don't forget me. But if you loose it and we part I still want to be in your heart!

November 24, 1938   Jude Markoff

Just like the golden rays of sun stretch proudly through the sky, may bright and happy sunny days stretch through your whole life.

The 10,000 Children That Hitler Missed

November 29, 1938   Hoffe Reich

Get to know the people, since they always change so fast. Today they call themselves your friends next week they talk behind your back!

December 19, 1938   Hanni Hockberg

If there is faith that can shift mountains, it is the faith in your own strength.

No date.   Ignats Irrsatz

As long as you are still a girl learn how to walk in storms. Turn with a slight smile to all the winds. Life comes in new hurricanes but you will see how strong you have grown.

February 24, 1938   Selma Millet

Don't talk too much and tell the truth, too many words won't do you good.

Victor and Regina Millet had two children: Selma and Alexander. They all died in the Holocaust.

April 11, 1938   Berta Bruder

If they ask you how you're feeling always answer: "good". While your friend will be happy to hear it, you'll bring your foes in a bad mood.

17: Sonja's Cherished Diary

April 28, 1938   Cousin Susi

Gold and silver I love a lot. But you, my dear Sonya, I love a thousand times more!

May 2, 1938   Alice Meier

Your Mothers tender hands were taking care of you and in your gentle heart they saved the seed of good. Remember this and always treat her with respect to love her is your duty and this you can't forget.

May 2, 1938   Inge Gottfried

The one who is striving for wisdom is wise. The one who believes to possess it is a fool!

May 10, 1938   Miriam Goldblatt

Don't ever judge a man whom you don't really know. Above are the choppy waves, the bottom is covered with pearls.

Barnda and Adel Goldblatt had Miriam in 1926. Miriam died in the Holocaust at the age of 16 in 1942.

May, 18, 1938   Helga Schnog

This line_____is mine! Remember me.

The 10,000 Children That Hitler Missed

Helga was born on March 5, 1925 to Moritz and Martha Schnog. Her younger sister was Ingrid. Helga and her father perished in Auschwitz while Martha and Ingrids whereabouts are unknown.

May 19, 1938   Charlotte Eppstein

May the man be noble, and helpful and good.

May 1938   Gisella Sonneman

One day we met each other. One day we'll have to part. Someday we'll meet again in the city of heaven.

May 1938   Lilu Tubar

Some day long distance will keep us apart. May the one who wrote you these words stay always in your heart.

May 25, 1938   Ilse Heidt

Be honest and open, don't ever neglect it. This way you can hope to be respected. In memory of the school years.

July 12, 1938   Senta Ehrenfeld

Reunion wasn't meant without separation no spring light would wake up without the winter snow. On stormy windy days think of the spring salvation and when we have to part think of the day we'll meet!

17: Sonja's Cherished Diary

July 19, 1938   Trudy Friedelmann

An album is a person's inner life that's kept in god's arms. An empty page is getting everyone. What you write there is what you are.

Trudy was born in 1926 and died in the Holocaust.

-1939-

The tone and temperament of the poems in 1939 began to shift to sorrow, goodbye messages, and hope that God would rescue them from the dangers of war. Fifteen children shared their thoughts in Sonja's diary. Sadly, their young eyes witnessed atrocities that no human should endure. They were a lost generation of children who never had an opportunity to live, dream, and be.

Each and every poem is endearing, yet one particular poem possesses a keen insight about the historical importance of the time. Chajor Gewurty wrote, "Know where you came from, where you are going to, and for whom you will have to remember the account one day." Chajor left on the Kindertransport and wrote as if she was addressing future generations. Indeed, she was. Out of the fifteen children who shared their poems in Sonja's diary in 1939, only one survived the Holocaust: Chajor Gewurty.

In 1939, Adolf Hitler was raging a fierce war against Europe and the Jews. On September 1, the Germans attacked Poland. Two days later, Britain and France declared war on Germany, and World War II in Europe officially began. Concurrently, Hitler proclaimed to the German Parliament that he intended to kill all European Jews. The ghettos were organized for Polish Jews, and the murder of millions of innocent people, including children, began unfolding. Persecution became more rampant and Jews all across Europe scrambled to find freedom in other countries. However, most never had the opportunity to leave or were not welcomed. Sadly, the tragedies of war and harassment got the better of so many.
Diary Entries 1939-

17: Sonja's Cherished Diary

January 1939   Martha

You are a Jew, remain a Jew share joy and sorrow with your people.

January 16, 1939   Martha Jakobowitz

When the storms are roaring, when you feel abandoned, raise your eyes and believe in the one who's always there.

March 5, 1939   Zogen

Think of me in Cologne on/Rhine.

March 16, 1939   Toni Ostro

You start with god, you end with god, and when you end with god you know you haven't erred.

March 16, 1939   Margot

May your happiness be bigger than a mountain, may your misfortune be smaller than a dwarf, may your future husband be a millionaire. Tell me, Sonya what else do you want?

March 1939   Esther Keeflik

This is your parents house. This is where you grew up. Soon you will start your own life. But this house should be in your heart!

No date   Ruth Levy

Life is a struggle, win it!

May 1939   Ellen Flogerhever

May your life be happy and sunny. May no sorrow sadden your heart. May happiness always be your companion. May you meet no grief on your path.

June 1939   Karla Levy

Why do you always long for the distance? See, the best is just nearby. Simply learn to catch your happiness because the happiness is always here.

July 1938   Walter Stern

We meet we give away our hearts we fall in love and have to part. Walter was born in 1925 and perished in the Holocaust.

No date   Friedel Frost

May your shadow never grow less!

July 6, no year   Mary Herschberg

17: Sonja's Cherished Diary

If I'm not for myself, who will be for me? If I am for myself only, who am I, If not how, when?

No date   Jenny Kuflin

When the moonlight fills your room think of me. I'll think of you!

August 25, 1939   Chajor Gewurtz

Know where you came from, where you are going to, and for whom you will have to remember the account one day. In fond memory of our moving to England.

November 24, 1939   Inge Elber

Even if a dream is lost, never lose the hope. Even if one door is closed thousands are still open.

Entries From Kindertransportees-

When the children first arrived on the Kindertrnasport, some were sent to Dovercourt Hardwich Holiday camp. The camp was close to the famous White Cliffs of Dover, making it an ideal spot for outdoor sports. In the interim, it was utilized as housing for the refugees because it was capable of housing large groups of children. Every Sunday, prospective parents would arrive to look over the children and decide which ones they wanted to take home with them. It was a rather humiliating situation for the children not chosen. Naturally the cute young children with smiling faces and adorable looks were

131

chosen right away while the others had to be sent to hostels. The chosen ones were often adopted temporarily by private families but ultimately sent back to their birth parents when the war was over.

Adjusting to their new lives in England was an emotional time for these youngsters. They were confused about why they were sent away without their families and simply could not understand why their parents could not board the train with them. Now, almost 70 years later, these questions still plague them. Why did Hitler have to hate us? Why was it bad to be Jewish? Why did I leave but my sister stayed behind? Why can't I pack my favorite doll? Why was daddy arrested? Why did they burn down the synagogue? Why did I have to wear this number tag around my neck? Why did I have to leave? Why? The questions flowed in their young minds like a reoccurring nightmare, but most never shared their thoughts out loud and their feelings became bottled up.

Most of the children corresponded with their parents and cherished the postcards and letters they received. Learning about their parents' safety reassured them. The very young children who couldn't write drew pictures for their parents, and some of the foster parents graciously sent postcards. The older children declared their love and affection while they desperately missed home and simply found it difficult at times to remain optimistic. The parents, on the other hand, did not want to worry their children and tried to send letters that were hopeful. As the war progressed, the letters from the parents became more revealing, and some pleaded for help while others even wrote their final farewells. Eventually the letters completely stopped because their

17: Sonja's Cherished Diary

parents were sent to concentration camps. The diary entries from the Kindertransport children give us a glimpse into their lives while they lived in exile.

Diary Entries 1940-

August 11, 1940   Margot

Do not isolate yourself from the community, don't have confidence in yourself until the day of your death. Don't judge your neighbor until you've walked one mile in his shoes.

Margot arrived on the Kindertransport on August 11, 1939. Eight years after her arrival she became a British citizen. It is believed that her parents were killed in the Holocaust. Today she resides in East Bartnet, a suburb of London. She is a nursery school teacher.

January 3, 1941   Eva

Not everyone who smiled has light behind their smile. Sometimes I have to laugh in order not to cry.

Eva was born on October 31, 1923 in Germany. She arrived in Britain on August 23, 1939, at sixteen years of age. In January of 1941, Eva lived at Gwrych Castle, in North East Wales where she slept on a straw mattress on the floor without electricity and contended with the castles deteriorating conditions. The castle was allocated to the Orthodox Youth Alyah however; it is unclear if Eva was an Orthodox Jew herself as some refugee at the castle weren't. Eva recalls her experience at Gwrych Castle as "hard but beautiful." Spoken like a true survivor even amongst the difficult circumstances. The Castle was led by Erwin Seligman a dedicated man with an intense commitment to the fellowship and the children.

17: Sonja's Cherished Diary

No date   Herthel

Always act and think like those, whose love and respect you want to earn. Do so every time you speak about people, even if they are not in your community. When you remember about all the nice things (and not so nice ones in the beginning) in the Kinnersley house, I belong there too.

Herthel remained in England and submitted a page of testimony in 1973 to the Yad Vashem (from the central database of Holocaust victims names) reporting the death of her parents, Max and Felix Flaschmann.

March 31, 1942   Margot

Remember often and kindly about the beautiful times at home and in Gwrych castle.

March 26, 1941   Edith P.

This is my farewell.

April 1, 1941   Regine

We are submerged in the Universe. We have contributed to the creation of the world order, or, since it has existed forever, we contributed even more. There are so many of us that the share of this contribution of each one of us is extremely small, that's why we are not aware of this contribution.

April 1, 1941   Mior S.

Those are the wise who travel from mistakes to the truth. The one who is mistaken remains a fool!

April 21, no year   Bella

In any situation only rely on yourself. Think about Gwyrch Castle and about our room thirteen.

August 11, 1940   Sabine

The one who shows you your mistakes, no matter if it hurts, the one who doesn't try to please you with careful choosing words. This person is your friend indeed, the one, who never lies. This friend is better than the one who fills you up with pride. Remember kindly about the time in Gwrych.

August 11, 1940   Joska

The man thinks God guides. Gwyrych Castle

August 11, 1940   Klara W.

You shouldn't say everything that you know, but you should know everything that your saying.

✯ ✯ ✯

17: Sonja's Cherished Diary

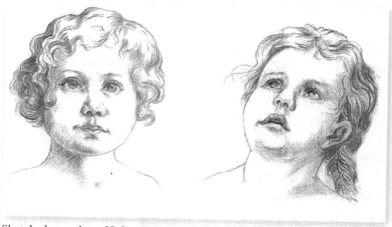

Sketch drawn by a Holocaust survivor while in the Theresienstadt concentration camp. The young girls depicted were killed in the Holocaust. (Courtesy Michael Williams)

Entry From Holocaust Survivor Friedel Kempler and her sister Nora-

January 14, 1939   Friedel Kempler (Theresienstadt survivor)

"Go do your thing, in silence and with faith, hack hogs hew stones, g-d our lord will build"

January 14, 1939   Nora Kempler (Friedel Kempler's younger sister, died in Auschwitz)

"Just like the sound of flute, So soft, so nice and clear, Just like the glow of sunshine, that's how your life should be!"

The 10,000 Children That Hitler Missed

Seven decades after writing her poem in Sonja's diary, Friedel was located residing in New York City as Rita Weissman. Today, she is an old woman and is surprised to hear about the diary that she and her sister Nora signed so many decades ago. She recalls, "I wanted to travel on the Kindertransport like some of my friends but was not chosen." As she reveals her personal struggle about her family during the Holocaust, she is haunted by the details and refrains from sharing the gory facts of her life. Her voice thickens and then quivers, her eyes fill with moisture, and she struggles to reveal even the smallest point. The pain and anguish are deeply buried in her heart and the slightest trigger brings all the terror back. She is slumped in her chair, hair white, face embedded with deep wrinkles. Recently released from the hospital, now in her eighties, this might be her final moment to reveal her untold story.

I was born in Germany to Joseph and Johanna Kempler. My parent married in 1923 and settled in Cologne, Germany, which lies at the Rhine. I was the oldest of five children: Issac, Willie, Nora, and Emil. My father, Joseph, was in the glacier business, a profession that had been carried down from several generations. We were a tight-knit family who attended the synagogue weekly and were committed to our Jewish roots. I was nine years old when Adolph Hitler became chancellor of Germany on January 30, 1933. Soon into his dictatorship, our once comfortable lives became inundated with anti-Semitism, restrictions, and curfews. Eventually, we were alienated in our own country and our God given rights became a luxury that we no longer possessed.

17: Sonja's Cherished Diary

On November 9, 1938, in the middle of the night, a loud bang erupted on the front door. *Bash, Bash!* My siblings and I were sleeping in the living room which happened to be our makeshift bedroom. The loud noise at the door startled everyone and we awakened. An SS man wearing a swastika cuffed around his arm entered our home. He screamed at my dad, "Joseph, get out, get out, get!" The Nazi's voice barked like a dog and cast loudly against the hollow walls. "Get out now!" We were shivering underneath our blankets. In one quick sweep, our father was forcibly pushed out of him home, his arm bent behind his back, a rifle digging into his spine. Without even a goodbye, a hug, or a kiss, he left us that day and we never saw him again. He was later killed in the Nowy Sach ghetto.

We were overcome with grief and soon realized that thousands of men were arrested that day and taken to concentration camps. Soon after my dad left, my mother invited another family (the Cohens) to reside with us to earn extra money. Subsequently, I tried to get on the Kindertransport list but was refused because they were only accepting German Jews and I was a Polish Jew. After the violence of Kristallnacht, my mother was persuaded by the Cohen family to allow me to go with them to Belgium to evade the atrocities that were unfolding. Desperate to save her family, my mom made the difficult decision to allow her 15-year-old to leave Germany. Unfortunately, she did not have the means to send my brothers and sisters as well, and they were simply too young.

My mother packed a suitcase for me. It included photographs of the family, scarves, mittens, and warm clothes. She hugged me with all her might and bid farewell. At the time, I did not realize that most of my family would be killed only a short time after I fled. I embraced my youngest brother Emil and teased him, "I am leaving because of you." He looked at me with his big round eyes and said in his high-pitched voice, "You are leaving because of Hitler!" Emil was three years old and was murdered in Auschwitz. Even young children were not spared from the evils of the Third Reich, and young Emil clearly knew how Hitler felt about Jews.

The Cohens and I departed in the middle of the night. We arrived on the outskirts of Belgium and paid a smuggler a hefty sum to escort us to safety. I soon settled into a new life and received a job as a live-in nanny and maid for a wealthy Jewish family that was in the diamond business. I took care of a young child, as I had experience caring for my brothers and sisters, but actually I was just a child myself.

When the Nazis invaded Belgium, my nanny position was terminated because the family flew to Paris. I pleaded to go with them but they refused and said that I would only get in the way. I lived in several different homes but was later arrested and sent to jail after refusing to work for the Germans. I was sent to five different prisons over a period of several years, but the Germans did not realize that I was a Jew, and I was simply imprisoned for not cooperating with them. Meanwhile, my family back home in Koln, Germany was forced to live

17: Sonja's Cherished Diary

in a ghetto and their lives were becoming more treacherous each day.

After enduring numerous penitentiaries, the Germans soon learned that I was Jewish. My life was about to take a turn for the worst. I was forced into a cattle car and endured a horrifying ride for many days with no food, no water, and no bathroom facility; the journey was torturous and many died en route. I arrived in Czechoslovakia at the Theresienstadt concentration camp. A large, arched sign bore the words, "Arbeit Macht Freit," which means "works brings freedom." I was put to work soon after my arrival, and my job was to split a rock called mica. I worked 12 hours a day, and despite the terrible living conditions, I was determined to keep my sanity. I vowed never to cry because "once you cried, you would grow weak, sick and die." Every day, hundreds died from starvation and disease. I simply shut down my feelings and dredged on in silence, yet with a determination to survive.

I observed the infamous glorification of the concentration camp as the Nazis prepared for the Red Cross visit. They carefully designed the transformation of the camp and shipped out hundreds of prisoners to empty out the facility. Suddenly, the camp was changed from a deplorable spectacle to an oasis, and onlookers would receive the deceit of a lifetime. The three-tiered bunks were pared down to two, and many new shops filled with food were showcased in the picture windows oozing with candy. Flowers were sprouted amongst the parks and lilies were planted along any bare soil. A playground with swing sets filled the sprawling park, and music pavilions with benches graced the outdoors. The visit from the Red Cross was deemed effective for the Nazis and they believe that the camp was rather nice and provided a wonderful occupancy for the Jews. The camouflage was successful, but little did they realize that the camp was actually a place of neglect, cruelty, and abuse, and most of the prisoners were sent to Nazi death camps in the east.

Subsequently, my mother and siblings were brought to Auschwitz, where Nora, Emil, and Johanna were sent to the gas chamber and murdered along with millions of other innocent people. The crematory in Auschwitz filled the sky with continuous smoke as lives were brutally taken away every second of every single minute for four long years. Izzy and Willie were used as forced labor and survived the brutality of Auschwitz, and they were liberated on January 27, 1945. They left Auschwitz different men. Their bodies were emaciated, their heads were shaved, their arms were tattooed with numbers, and they were clinging to the thin threads of life.

In 1945, Theresienstadt was liberated by the Russian Army. I recall one soldier calling out a women's name in a loud urging voice. He repeatedly reiterated this name, but no one answered. Soon, the soldier located the mystery woman and embraced her dearly with tears streaming down both their faces. Apparently, it was his grandmother and she never answered because she was deaf, but, miraculously, she survived the camp and they marveled in their reunion. Upon liberation, only 17,320

17: Sonja's Cherished Diary

prisoners were found alive, a fraction of the 140,000 who once occupied its walls.

I desperately wanted to go home, so I approached a Polish army liberator and urged him to help. The gentleman gave me a women's army uniform and I pinned my hair up and quickly put the uniform on. I traveled with the others who happened to be on their way to Germany, and no one suspected a thing. Upon arrival, I found the shell of my home standing in ruins. Germany was unrecognizable, my building was torn to the ground, rubble filled the streets, and whole neighborhoods were completely demolished. I went to the local hospital to look for my family or friends but found no one. The city was nothing like the town I had left behind, and it became apparent to me that my life along with many others was forever changed by the Holocaust and World War II.

I later learned that Izzy and Willie both survived Auschwitz, but the rest of my family had been killed. I reunited with Izzy, but we never shared the particulars of our lives in a concentration camp, as it was simply too painful to reiterate. Deep down, we both knew what we had gone through. At liberation, Izzy and Willie separated and planned on meeting back in Poland. Once Izzy got to Poland, he looked for Willie but he never found him. Although they survived the most vicious existence in Auschwitz, Willie never made it back to Poland, and we can only wonder what happened to him. I have spent my whole life trying to locate Willie, and I hope that before my dying day we will be reunited.

Friedel (now Rita Weissman) immigrated to the United States and settled in New York City. She married an American, bore a son, and is currently a widow but has been blessed with grandchildren. Izzy married and raised a family of his own. He died in the 1980s. Friedel sits in her wheelchair surrounded by pictures of her deceased family and remembers the grief and anguish that the Nazis caused for so many. Although Friedel does not remember Sonja Herzberg, she does recall signing the diary.

TIMELINE OF EVENTS

October 31, 1924 Sonya Herzberg was born to Leopold and Regina Herzberg.

March 10, 1933 Michael, a prosperous Jewish attorney was beaten on the streets of Munich by storm troopers and forced to wear a sign, "I am a Jew, but I will never complain to the police."

April 23, 1933, Franz was dismissed from his position as a Judge in Germany since he was half-Jewish.

June 6, 1933 Anita Hoffer was born in Berlin, Germany five months prior Adolf Hitler was named chancellor of Germany.

May 1936 fascist Italy invaded Ethiopia and Haile Selassie and his family fled to London.

1937 Sonya Herzberg began her little blue diary.

March 1938 Germany invades Austria and Hugo Schneider's dental practice is seized by the Nazis.

May 10, 1938 Miriam Goldblatt inscribed a poem in Sonya Herzberg's diary at age 12; she was murdered four years later.

May 18, 1938 Helga Schog declared her poem to Sonya Herzberg at age 13. Several years later she was gassed in Auschwitz.

May 19, 1938 Helga Salm wrote in Sonyas's diary, "Forget the hours of trouble but never forget what they have taught you!

October 1938 the Alpern family was sent to Zbonsyn a refugee camp on the boarder of Poland and Germany, the conditions were terrible and many committed suicide

November 9, 1938 Joseph Kempler was arrested by the Nazis during Kristallnach with 30,000 other victims.

November 21, 1938 the Kindertransport was officially launched!

1938 Alfred Terry secured his own passport at the tender age of 11 then embarked on the Kindertransport.

November 21, 1938 the first Kindertransport train leaves Berlin and arrives in the Liverpool, Hardwick Station.

1938 Edith Mollerick was given a prayer book by her mother before she departed to England. On Edith's death bed in 1987, she gave the cherished book to her brother Ralph and he still possesses it today.

Timeline of Events

1938 the Nazis boarded the Kindertransport train near the German/Dutch frontier and terrorized the children with frightful threats. The Nazis declared that they would seize any valuables and sent the train back if they located any expensive items. Alfred Terry recalls the children bawling, yet in the end, no search was ever conducted; they simply wanted to bully the children.

December 17, 1938 Lisa and Peter Seiden left Vienna on the Kindertransport and arrived in England.

January 19, 1938 Lisa Seiden is welcomed at the St. Marks School in England with hugs, kisses and compassion, from the other students.

January 4, 1939 Inga and Isle Lichtenstein traveled to the Netherlands on the Kindertransport and endured a twelve hour trip.

August 23, 1939 Sonya Herzberg arrived in Britain on the Kindertransport at the age of fifteen.

August 25, 1939 Chajor Gewurty wrote a revealing poem in Sonya's diary, "Know where you came from where you are going to, and for whom you will have to remember the account one day."

September 1, 1939 Manfred Alweiss arrived in England on the last transport before the war was declared.

The 10,000 Children That Hitler Missed

February 15, 1939 The Alpern family was sent to England to start a new life. The newspapers documented their story because they were the only complete family to arrive on the Kindertransport.

May 1939 Thirty-four students including Julius Fleischer (now Fletcher) fled on the Kindertransport while all were over the age limit of 17.

June 27, 1939 Elizabeth and Lux arrived in England three months later the war broke out in England.

May 1940 Inga Lichtenstein's foster family in the Netherlands shipped her back to Germany to avoid the surging war. She died two years later with her parents.

1942 Ralph and Edith Mollerick learn that their parents were taken to Lodz, Poland which served as a holding area prior to shipment to Auschwitz. Sadly, they were murdered.

1942 Alfred Terry's parents were forced into a cattle car, traveled without food or water and suffered a torturous ride. Upon arrival in Minsk they were killed.

Ellen and Inga Bottner were reunited with their parents in the winter of 1945 the reunion was bittersweet.

Franz became a Judge in 1949 fifteen years earlier his position as a Judge was revoked because he was part Jewish.

Timeline of Events

January 18, 1949 Sonya Herzberg age 25 immigrated to Israel.

1955 Ilse Lichtenstein married Meinhard Mayer a childhood friend from Germany. They both lost their family in the Holocaust.

1976 Ellen and Inga Bottner visited England 37 years after their arrival on the Kindertransport the trip was long overdue and they cherished every moment of it.

2006 Friedel Kempler a Holocaust survivor from Theresienstadt was found living as Rita Weissman in New York City. Seven decades before, she shared a friendship with Sonja Herzberg, and declared a poem along with her sister Nora. Sadly, Nora, and most of their family was murdered in the Holocaust.

POSTSCRIPT

Britain has shown us that freedom of humanity can never be extinguished. Although the incomprehensible horror and cruelty engulfed the masses, the love and generosity of others proves that hope can prevail and life can triumph the atrocities of the deplorable acts cast upon humanity during the Holocaust. The people of Britain are selfless humanitarians, and today we see the fruits from their sacrifices. Without their compassion, sympathy, bravery, and heroism, brutality would have swept up the children into the black hole of Nazism.

We remember the stories not to deliberately open hurtful wounds, not to torment the next generation with painful memories. We remember as part of our homage to the victims. If we fail the victims, then their horrific suffering and death will have no great meaning. We must commit to emancipate racial and religious hatred and to eradicate oppression and cruelty. We need to purge our hearts of all hatred that creeps into our minds. We are all God's children.

Taking the painful walk with survivors evokes emotions in all of us, and, it opens a dialogue about hate and persecution. Sonja's diary should serve as a reminder that innocent children can be targeted by hate because hate has no boundaries, no guidelines or limitations. When children are thrown alive into ovens, sheer madness has prevailed, and the ugliness of hatred has emerged. The children who declared their sweet poems in Sonja's diary never has an opportunity to flourish, grow, and blossom into the miraculous beings God intended them to be. They were murdered ruthlessly just because of their religious beliefs. Sonja's friends expressed their desire to believe in the future and move past the dark days that encompassed their lives. On January 16, 1939 Martha Jakobowitz shared this message of hope in Sonja's diary: "When the storms are roaring, when you feel abandoned, raise your eyes and believe in the one who's always there". Sadly, she was murdered in the Holocaust. Anne Frank also expressed her desire to end violence and hateful actions. She hoped that peace would soon return again.

Each and every survivor's story was gathered with love, respect, and compassion and I am truly grateful that they have trusted me to be their messenger. Their stories represent a time in history that must be remembered, studied, embraced, and analyzed. It must also serve as a vehicle to end violence against humanity. We must never forget the atrocities perpetrated by mankind and endured by innocent victims, ordinary men, women, and children. We need to plead for decency, strengthen our moral obligations, and stand up for human rights.

In the end, the survivors seemed to develop astonishing resilience: on the other hand, it left them searching through the rubble to find meaning from an event that defies any meaning at all. Surprisingly, some never really knew the detailed account surrounding their parents' deaths. The unsettling murders will continue to plague

Postscript

us all. The victims were forsaken by a ruthless man who stood for evil and carried no remorse for his actions. Adolf Hitler could be regarded as a man who lived on earth but represented all that is associated with hell.

CREDITS AND SOURCES:

Bentwich, Norman. They Found Refuge. London: The Cresset Press, 1959

Frank, Anne, Otto H. Frank, and Mirjam Pressler. The Diary Of Anne Frank. 5th ed. New York: Doubleday, 1995.

Heide, Dirk Van Der. My Sister and I. 6th ed. New York: Harcourt Brace and Company, 1941.

Hertzburg, Sonja. Excerpts from her unpublished diary. Translated from German to English by Anastasia Sierra. Sonja's diary is available at: 19 Macarthur Drive Millbury, Ma. 01527.

Leverton, Berta. ed. "Special Interest Section". Kindertransport Newsletter Jan. (2004). 12 Sept. 2006.

Leverton, Berta. ed. "Special Interest Section". Kindertransport Newsletter Sept. (2005). 30 Jan. 2007.

"Photo Archives". United States Holocaust Museum. USHMM. 10 Jan. 2007 <http://www.ushmm.org/ula-cgi/uia-query.com>

"Photo Archives". United States Holocaust Museum. USHMM. 20 Jan. 2007 <http//www.ushmm.org/uia-cgi/uia_doc/photos/5219?hr=null.com>

"Photo Archives". <u>United States Holocaust Museum.</u> USHMM 29 Jan. 2007 <http//www.ushmm.org/uia_cgi/uia_doc/photos/10419?hr=null>

"Photo Archives". <u>United States Holocaust Museum.</u> USHMM 30 Jan 2007 <http//www.ushmm.org/uia_cgi/uia_doc/photos/7417?hr=null>

"Photo Archives". <u>United States Holocaust Museum.</u> USHMM 1 Feb 2007 <www.ushmm.org/uia_cgi_/uia_doc/photos/11927?hr=null.com>

Read, Sue <u>The Children Who Cheated The</u> Nazis, Golden Reed Productions Ltd.

✭ ✭ ✭

ADDITIONAL RESOURCES:

The 10,000 Children That Hitler Missed Speak Out
www.holocaustkinder.com

Kindertransport Association, Inc. (KTA)
www.kindertransport.org

Survivors of the Shoah Visual History Foundation
www.vhf.org

United States Holocaust Memorial Museum
100 Raoul Wallenburg Place SW
Washington, DC 20024
www.ushmm.org

"The Views or opinions expressed in this book and the context in which the images are used, do not necessarily reflect the views or policy of, nor imply approval or endorsement by, the United States Holocaust Museum".

The author has endeavored to identify the current copyright owner of the selections in this book and to obtain permission to include them, whenever necessary. In the event of an error or omission in my acknowledgement, please contact the author through the publisher and, if appropriate, and feasible, an acknowledgement will be included in future printings.

✵ ✵ ✵

Made in the USA
Lexington, KY
05 January 2017